WORLD FAMOUS SCANDALS

WORLD FAMOUS
SCANDALS

Colin Wilson
with Damon and Rowan Wilson

SIENA

This is a Siena Book
Siena is an imprint of Parragon Book Service Ltd
Produced by Magpie Books 1996
First published by Magpie Books,
an imprint of Robinson Publishing Ltd, 1992

Robinson Publishing Ltd
7 Kensington Church Court
London W8 4SP

British Library Cataloguing-in-Publication Data
A catalogue record for this book is available
from the British Library

ISBN 0 75251 623 X

Illustrations courtesy of Popperfoto
Cover pictures: Richard Nixon, Associated Press/Topham,
Oscar Wilde and Lord Alfred Douglas, Topham

Printed and Bound in the EC

Contents

Chapter one: **Sex Scandals**
Colonel Valentine Baker: Attempted Rape
  on a Train   1
The Cleveland Street Scandal: The "Sex-for-Sale"
  Telegraph Boys   7
Henry Ward Beecher: The Preacher and the
  Adoring Disciples   13
John Hugh Smyth Pigott: The "Abode of Love"
  Scandal   25
Fatty Arbuckle: A Star's Disgrace   28

Chapter two: **Financial Scandals**
Scotland Yard: The Great Bribery Scandal   35
Teapot Dome Scandal: The Ohio Gang
  Hijacks America   43
The "Suicide" of Roberto Calvi   48
Thérèse Humbert: the Impecunious Millionaire   56

Chapter three: **Literary Fraud**
Mikhail Sholokhov: The Quiet Flows the Don
  Plagiarism Scandal   63
Lobsang Rampa: The "Third Eye" Hoax   67
Carlos Castaneda: The Don Juan Hoax   72
William Henry Ireland: the Second Shakespeare   79

Chapter four: **How Have the Mighty Fallen**
Heinrich Schliemann: The Great Troy Hoax   85
Oscar Wilde: "One must seek out what
  is most tragic"   92
Ivor Novello: The Red Rolls-Royce Scandal   101
"Professor" C.E.M. Joad: The Rail Ticket Scandal   107

Chapter five: **Political Scandals**
Wilhelm Voigt: "The Captain from Kopenick"   114
President John F. Kennedy: All the President's
    Women   116
The Profumo Scandal   124
Jeremy Thorpe: Did the Liberal Leader hire a
    Hitman?   134
President Richard Milhous Nixon: The
    Watergate Break-in Scandal   141

Chapter six: **Royal Embarrassments**
Queen Caroline: The Only British Queen
    to be Tried for Adultery   149
The Baccarat Scandal: The Tranby Croft Case   154
The Buckingham Palace Security Scandal   158
Queen Victoria: The haemophiliac gene   165
Queen Victoria and John Brown   166

Chapter seven: **They Lost a Fortune**
Leona and Harry Helmsley   171
William Randolph Hearst   176

Chapter One

Sex Scandals

S *ex Scandals have occurred throughout the ages and no one is immune. A colonel attempts to rape a girl who has rebuffed him, a star who believes he is irresistible thinks any woman will want to be with him, and a "prophet" endorses free love — who has significantly more women in the congregation than men . . .*

Colonel Valentine Baker — Attempted Rape on a Train

The attempt of Colonel Valentine Baker to rape a young lady on a train was one of the most widely publicized scandals of the 1870s.

On the afternoon of 17 June 1875, a 21-year-old girl named Rebecca Kate Dickinson boarded the Portsmouth to London train at Midhurst, in Sussex. She was alone in the compartment when 49-year-old Colonel Valentine Baker, until recently commanding officer of the 10th Hussars, entered the train at Liphook. Miss Dickinson was a pretty, self-possessed young lady who was on her way to Switzerland for a holiday. Colonel Baker was Assistant Quartermaster-General at Aldershot, a highly distinguished soldier who was an intimate friend of the Prince of Wales. He was also a married man, with two young daughters.

Baker made polite conversation for the first fifty minutes of the journey, apparently the ultra-respectable English gentleman exchanging commonplaces with a girl young enough to be his daughter or even granddaughter. But when the train pulled out of Woking, and London was half an hour away, he suddenly asked her if she often travelled alone. When she said she didn't, he asked her if they could meet on the train at some future time. She said no. He asked her name and she declined to tell him. He asked if he could write to her and she said no. He then closed the window and sat down next to her. When she asked him to sit further away he said, "Don't be cross", and put his arm round her waist. "You must kiss me, darling." She struggled to her feet but he forced her down again and held her down with his weight while he kissed her again and again on the lips. "If I give you my name will you get off?" she asked. Instead of replying he sank in front of her, thrust one hand up her dress and began to fumble with his flies with the other.

She struggled to her feet and tried to smash the window with her elbow; then she lowered it and screamed. Baker pulled her back so violently that she was half suffocated. She twisted the door handle and began to climb out backwards. "Get in, dear!" said the Colonel in great alarm. And he offered to get out of the other door in an effort to calm her. But she knew the other door was locked.

She could see two men looking out of the window of the next compartment as she balanced on the running board and she shouted, "How long before the train stops?" But their answer was carried away by the roar of the engine and the wind.

At 4.45 the train passed through Walton station and a bricklayer called William Burrowes saw a young lady standing on the running board, clinging to the handle of the door; someone inside the compartment seemed to be preventing her from falling by holding on to her other arm. The stationmaster signalled to Esher and there the train stopped. As it began to slow down, Baker said urgently, "Don't say anything — you don't know what trouble you'll get me into. Say you were frightened."

Railway officials at Esher wanted to know what had happened but she was too upset and exhausted to say much. Baker was told to go into another compartment. A clergyman named Baldwin Brown got in with Miss Dickinson and travelled with her to London.

At Waterloo, Miss Dickinson, Colonel Baker and the Reverend Brown were taken to the Inspector's office. Baker must have been relieved when she declined to go into details about her complaint. She gave her name and address; so did Baker. And then the Reverend Brown escorted her to her brother's house – he was a doctor living in Chesterfield Street. At this point, Rebecca Dickinson apparently wanted to forget the whole thing but her brother pointed out that Baker might do the same thing to other girls. So, reluctantly, she agreed to report the matter to the police.

The news items about the case caused widespread interest and astonishment. Valentine Baker was the kind of soldier who had created the British Empire; he was also the author of a number of books on cavalry tactics. He was the younger brother of the explorer Sir Samuel Baker, who had journeyed to the source of the Nile. It was true that he was the son of a merchant, not a "gentleman", but the Victorian era was the age of opportunity, and no one held this against him, least of all the future King Edward VII, his close friend. Surely there must be some mistake? Why should such a man risk his career and reputation to assault a girl on a train?

Three days after the assault, Baker was arrested at Guildford. His trial took place at Croydon Assizes on 2 August 1875, a Bank Holiday Monday. Huge crowds gathered outside the courtroom long before the trial was due to start at 10.30 a.m. Two well-dressed ladies even tried to get in through a window. Many peers were in court, including Lord Lucan and the Marquess of Tavistock. A rumour was going about that those in "high places" had arranged for the whole thing to be dropped, so there was some relief when the Grand Jury found a True Bill and Mr Justice Brett refused to postpone the trial. There was so much noise coming from the crowds outside – disappointed at being unable to get in – that the case had to be adjourned for ten minutes while the police tried to restore order. Then Mr Sergeant Parry, QC, for the prosecution, called Miss Dickinson into the witness box. But he declined to increase her distress by asking her a single question. So the defence lawyer, Henry Hawkins, cross-examined her. He elicited the interesting fact that part of the conversation between Liphook and Woking had been about hypnotism and that Colonel Baker had told Miss Dickinson that he thought she could be mesmerized. She also detailed other topics they had discussed, including the murder of a certain Mr Walker. The defence was obviously trying to establish that Miss Dickinson's openness, her willingness to engage in animated conversation, had probably convinced the Colonel that a kiss might not be rejected.

But the evidence against the Colonel was serious. He had fairly certainly intended rape – otherwise, why had he unbuttoned his flies? The guard had noticed that they were undone at Esher. And so had the two gentlemen in the carriage that Baker transferred into. He had also put his hand up her skirt, although it had apparently gone no further than above the top of her boot.

The judge's summing up emphasized that Baker's chief concern had apparently been to save Miss Dickinson from falling from the running board and he indicated that he could see no evidence that there was "intent to ravish". This was on the grounds that Baker had hoped to win the girl's consent to intercourse by "exciting her passions". The jury took the hint. Baker was found not guilty of intent to ravish but guilty of indecent assault and common assault. The judge then told Baker sternly that, "Of all the people who travelled in the train that day, you were the most bound to stand by and defend a defenceless woman. Your crime is as bad as it could be." And he sentenced Baker to a year in jail – without hard labour – and a fine of £500.

The Press, on the whole, felt it was a just verdict — most people had believed that this friend of royalty would be acquitted. But the general public seemed to feel that Baker had got off too easily — a mere year in "honourable detention", then back to the old life.

But Baker was disgraced. He tried to resign his commission and was told that he was to be cashiered. It was widely believed that this was due to Queen Victoria's intervention. (The Queen was not fond of her rakish son — or his friends.) It is true that, in Horsemonger Lane jail, Baker was treated with due consideration, allowed to wear his own clothes, to send out for his food and to receive his friends more or less as he wished. But the knowledge that he had involved his family in the most degrading kind of public scandal was enough to turn him into a psychological wreck. Three months after his imprisonment, it was reported that he was critically ill. *The Times* published a letter from his wife assuring his "many friends" that he was no longer in danger of his life but admitting that his condition caused her much distress.

He served his full term; then, with his wife and two young daughters he left England. He became a lieutenant-general in the Ottoman army and fought bravely during the Russo-Turkish war. Then he went to Egypt and accepted an appointment as a commander of police. He attempted unsuccessfully to relieve Tokar during the Sudan war but his poorly trained force was destroyed. He himself was seriously wounded in a later action. When he came back to London to recuperate, a cheering crowd greeted him at Victoria Station. His friends tried hard to get him reinstated in the British army. But their efforts were a failure — almost certainly due to Queen Victoria's determination that the would-be rapist would never again become a soldier of the queen. Baker died of heart failure, after an attack of typhoid, on 12 November 1887, twelve years after the Dickinson case. The Queen finally relented and cabled that Baker was to be buried in Cairo with full military honours.

The mystery remains: why did Baker do it? In court he swore solemnly that the facts were not as Miss Dickinson represented them. His supporters took this to mean that she had given him some encouragement. He also spoke of her "exaggerated fear". Did he mean that he believed she had been willing to be kissed but had become alarmed when he had shown signs of being carried away?

But the theory that Baker gave way to an "irresistible impulse" will not hold water. He was a highly disciplined soldier and discipline means the ability to resist "impulses". Yet this in itself suggests another explanation. Baker was a close friend of the Prince of Wales who spent much of his time bedding attractive women. So it is easy to understand that Baker may have regarded Rebecca Dickinson as a challenge, the natural prey of a dashing cavalry officer. But when he asked her if he might see her again, he was promptly rebuffed. For a man who is accustomed to giving orders and having them obeyed – and probably dominating his own wife and daughters with the natural authority of a sultan – this must have seemed an intolerable humiliation. He might have withdrawn stiffly into his shell and passed the rest of the journey to London in sulky silence. But he was not that kind of a man; he was used to pressing on in the face of odds. He asked her name and again was rebuffed. The distinguished soldier, the friend of royalty, was being snubbed by a mere "chit of a girl". By this time he was probably burning with humiliation – and with the feeling that perhaps, after all, he was making a fool of himself. The author of a book on cavalry tactics had mistimed his charge. If he drew back now, he would remember this for the rest of his life with a shock of outraged vanity. The soldier had to act. He stood up and closed the window . . .

Cleveland Street Scandal – The "Sex-for-Sale" Telegraph Boys

In early July 1889, there was a theft of money from a room in the General Post Office in St Martin's-Le-Grand, in the City of London. A telegraph messenger boy named Charles Thomas Swinscow came under suspicion and when he was searched, he proved to have eighteen shillings on him – a far larger sum than he was likely to save up from his wages. On 4 July 1889, a police constable named Hanks questioned the boy, who told him that he had obtained the money for doing some "private work" for a gentleman named Hammond, who lived at 19 Cleveland Street, just north of Soho. Finally, he admitted that he had been taken to the house by a post office clerk named Henry Newlove – who, like Swinscow, was fifteen. Newlove, it seemed, had earlier

Georges Simenon, the creator of Inspector Maigret, caused widespread consternation in 1974 when he told a Swiss journalist during an interview that he had had sex with ten thousand women. He expanded on this in his book *Intimate Memoirs*, explaining that about eight thousand of these had been prostitutes. In his biography of Simenon, Fenton Bresler describes how Simenon had his first sexual encounter at the age of twelve – with a girl of sixteen – and how, in later life, he obsessively sought out prostitutes in every place he visited. Yet Bresler admits that Simenon's claim is probably exaggerated. Even at a rate of a woman a day, ten thousand would require thirty years, without a day off . . .

persuaded Swinscow to go with him to a lavatory in the basement of the Post Office where he had "behaved indecently". Then Newlove had suggested that Swinscow might like to earn a little money by doing the same thing with a gentleman. At the house in Cleveland Street, Swinscow had got into bed with a gentleman who, in the language of the police report, "put his person between my legs and an emission took place". The gentleman then gave him half a sovereign, which Swinscow handed to the landlord of the house, Hammond. Hammond had given him back four shillings. The same thing had apparently happened on a subsequent occasion.

Swinscow mentioned two other telegraph boys who had gone to Cleveland Street: seventeen-year-olds George Wright and Charles Thickbroom. Wright admitted that he and Newlove had gone to the basement lavatory and "Newlove put his person into me . . . and something came away from him." Wright went with Newlove to the Cleveland Street house where he went to a bedroom with a "foreign looking chap". They undressed and got into bed. "He had a go between my legs and that was all." Wright also received four shillings. Thickbroom told how Newlove had persuaded him to go to Cleveland Street, where he went to bed with a gentleman and they "played with one another. He did not put his person into me." He also received four shillings.

Newlove admitted the truth of the statements. The next morning he hastened to 19 Cleveland Street and warned Hammond. Charles Hammond, a 32-year-old male prostitute, married to a French prostitute known as "Madame Caroline" – on whom he had fathered two sons – lost no time in fleeing. So did another homosexual, George Veck, who liked to pose as a clergyman. Veck moved to lodgings nearby under a false name, while Hammond fled to France.

Chief Inspector Frederick Abberline of the CID applied for warrants for the arrest of Hammond and Newlove on a

charge of criminal conspiracy. But when the police arrived
at Cleveland Street the next day the house was shut up.

On his way to the police station, Newlove commented
that it was hard that he should be arrested when men in
high positions should be allowed to walk free. Asked what
he meant, he replied, "Lord Arthur Somerset goes regularly
to the house in Cleveland Street. So does the Earl of Euston
and Colonel Jervois."

Lord Arthur Somerset, the son of the Duke of Beaufort,
was a major in the Royal Horse Guards, and superintendent
of the stables of the Prince of Wales, Queen Victoria's son,
whose name was to be associated with many scandals
(including the Tranby Croft card scandal). When Lord
Arthur — known as "Podge" — was identified by the two
telegraph boys Swinscow and Thickbroom as the man who
had climbed into bed with them, "Podge" hastily obtained
four months' leave of absence and vanished to the Continent. His elder brother Henry had been deserted by his
wife because of his homosexual inclinations.

Veck was also arrested and he and Newlove were
committed for trial at the Old Bailey. But by that time,
the press had got hold of the story. The *Pall Mall Gazette*
published a paragraph deploring the "disgraceful nature" of
the charge against Veck and Newlove and asking whether
the "two noble lords and other notable persons in society"
were going to be allowed to get away with it. It obviously
had the makings of a first-class scandal. It may have been at
this point that Arthur Newton, "Podge's" solicitor,
breathed another name that made the Director of Public
Prosecutions raise his eyebrows: that of "Eddy", the Duke
of Clarence, son of the Prince of Wales. Eddy, according to
rumour, had also visited the Cleveland Street brothel.
Meanwhile, "Podge" was in more trouble; another teen-
ager, Algernon Allies, had been interviewed by the police
and admitted that he had been intimately involved with
Lord Arthur Somerset, whom he called "Mr Brown". "The

prosecution wishes to avoid putting any witness in the box who refers to 'Mr Brown'," wrote the Director of Public Prosecutions, Sir Augustus Stephenson to the Attorney-General.

It was no surprise to anyone when the case came up at Bow Street on 18 September 1889 and lasted a mere half hour. Veck and Newlove both pleaded guilty and were both given light sentences. Veck, nine months' hard labour and Newlove, four months'. That, it seemed, was the end of the case.

But the Press was not willing to allow it to rest there. There were many crusading editors in London, like W.T. Stead of the *Pall Mall Gazette*, Henry Labouchere of *Truth*, and Ernest Parke of the *North London Press*. It was Parke who put the cat among the pigeons. On 16 November 1889 Parke identified the aristocrats whose names had been so carefully suppressed at the time of the trial: Lord Arthur Somerset and the Earl of Euston. (These names, we may recall, had been mentioned to Abberline by Newlove when he was arrested.) Parke also commented that "a far more distinguished and more highly placed personage . . . was inculpated in these disgusting crimes."

The Earl of Euston, Henry James Fitzroy, was thirty-eight years old at the time of the Cleveland Street trial. He immediately instructed his solicitor to sue for libel. Parke's trial opened at the Old Bailey on 15 January 1890. One of the most serious points against Parke was his allegation that the Earl of Euston had fled to Peru; Euston had done nothing of the sort. (It had been unnecessary, for his name had never entered the case after Newlove mentioned it to Abberline.)

Euston admitted that he had been to 19 Cleveland Street. But, he said, it had been a misunderstanding. He had, he said, been in Piccadilly in May or June 1889, when someone had put an advertising card into his hand. It said *"Poses plastiques"*, and gave the address of 19 Cleveland Street.

Poses plastiques meant naked girls posing in Grecian attitudes. So, according to Lord Euston, he hurried to 19 Cleveland Street. He was admitted by a man who told him there were no women there but left no doubt about what the house had to offer. "You infernal scoundrel, if you don't let me out I'll knock you down," said Lord Euston and rushed out.

The defence called several witnesses who said they had seen Lord Euston going in or out of Cleveland Street. The final defence witness was a male prostitute named John Saul. He claimed to have been picked up by Lord Euston who took him back to Cleveland Street where they went to bed. *The Times* declined to report what Saul claimed then took place but we can reconstruct what he said from a comment Saul had made to Ernest Parke about Euston: "He is not an actual sodomite. He likes to play with you and then 'spend' on your belly."

The judge emphasized the contradictions in the statements of witnesses, and described Saul as a "loathsome object". The strongest point against Parke was his statement that Euston had fled to Peru. The jury found Parke guilty of libel without justification. He was sentenced to a year in prison without hard labour. The sentence was not regarded as severe by the Press.

The case was still not quite over. In December 1889, "Podge's" solicitor, Arthur Newton, was accused of conspiring to defeat the course of justice. The charges said that he had tried to get an interview with Algernon Allies – the youth who had admitted being "Podge's" lover – and had collected three of the accused telegraph boys after they had left police custody and sent them to a lodging house while he arranged for them to leave the country. Newton's defence was that his clerk Frederick Taylorson, who was charged with him, had met Allies by accident and exchanged a few words with him. And as to the second charge, it was true that he had sent the three boys to a lodging house overnight, telling them that they ought to go abroad, but that this was because "Podge's" father, the Duke of Beaufort, wanted to interview them to see if they had been bullied by the police. The Duke had subsequently changed his mind. Newton was, he admitted, therefore technically guilty of conspiracy. The judge took a light view of it and sentenced him to six weeks in prison. Taylorson, who pleaded not guilty, was acquitted.

Hammond, the man who ran the brothel, had fled from France to America and was never tried. "Podge" spent the rest of his life living abroad, under an assumed name, and died in Hyères, on the French Riviera, in 1926. The scandal undoubtedly ruined his life. In his book *The Cleveland Street Scandal*, H. Montgomery Hyde suggests that he would have been wise to return and "face the music"; a good solicitor could also certainly have secured his acquittal, as in the case of Lord Euston. (The evidence suggests that Euston was a regular visitor at Cleveland Street.) Euston's trial certainly did him no harm; at the time of the Cleveland Street case he was a prominent Freemason, the Provincial Grand Master of Northamptonshire and Huntingdonshire, and subsequently became Grand Master of the Mark Masons. He was also appointed an aide de camp by King Edward VII in the coronation year, 1901. He died of dropsy in 1912.

Ernest Parke became a Justice of the Peace after he retired as a newspaper editor. But the subsequent career of Arthur Newton, who went to prison for conspiracy, was less fortunate. In 1910 he defended the murderer Crippen and received much favourable publicity. But he then conceived the idea of forging a Crippen "confession" and selling it to a newspaper: *The Evening Times* bought it for £500, the writer Edgar Wallace acting as a go-between. Although Newton got cold feet at the last moment, the newspaper forced him to deliver the promised confession and sold a million copies as a result. Newton was suspended from practice by the

Law Society for unprofessional conduct. In 1913 he was charged with being involved in a Canadian timber fraud, sentenced to three years in jail, and struck off the rolls as a solicitor.

Henry Ward Beecher –
The Preacher and the Adoring Disciples

Beecher was one of the most celebrated preachers of the nineteenth century. He was almost ruined by a scandal in which he was accused of adultery with one of his flock.

The Reverend Horatio Alger was one of the most popular of American authors in the late nineteenth century; his "rags to riches" success stories, with titles like *Dan the Newsboy* and *Paul the Peddler*, sold in vast numbers. He was also widely respected as the devoted head of the Newsboys' Lodging House in New York. What no one knew at the time was that Alger was a pederast, and that in 1864 (when he was thirty) he had been forced to hastily resign his position as pastor of the Unitarian Church of Brewster (Cape Cod) when the church committee learned that he had been buggering the choirboys. Alger left town before he could be arrested, and the committee was too embarrassed to publicize the matter.

Two years later he was made chaplain of Newsboys', and devoted the rest of his life to the care of young boys . . .

Scandals

Henry Ward was born in Litchfield, Connecticut, USA in June 1813, the eighth of thirteen children of the Reverend Lyman Beecher. He had been a shy child with a stammer and his scholastic performance had been abysmal until he went to Amherst College at the age of seventeen. At twenty-four he became minister to a small congregation at Lawrenceburg, Indiana, and began to develop his preaching talent. He was fundamentally an actor: he preferred to stand or sit on a platform rather than in a pulpit and told anecdotes with a wealth of gesture and facial expression that made his audience feel they were in a theatre. On one occasion, he mimed catching a fish so perfectly that a man in the front row jumped up crying, "By God, he's got him!" Physically speaking, Beecher was not unusually attractive, with a round face, thick lips, a fleshy nose and shoulder-length hair. But his congregation found him magnetic and women adored him. A book of his called *Seven Lectures to Young Men* appeared in 1844 and became something of a bestseller. Yet for many years he was regarded simply as one of the preacher-sons of the far more famous Lyman Beecher. In 1847, he was persuaded to move east by Henry C. Bowen, a Brooklyn businessman, whose young wife was an admirer of Beecher. Within three years, his sermons were attracting audiences of more than 2,000, and he had the largest congregation in America.

As he grew older, Beecher gradually changed his stance from that of a narrow, hell-fire revivalist preacher to a liberal who advocated women's rights and Darwinian evolutionism, and opposed slavery. In 1861, Bowen made Beecher the editor of his newspaper *The Independent*. A young man named Theodore Tilton, who passionately admired Beecher, had been given the job of managing editor, largely due to Beecher's insistence. In 1855, Beecher had married Theodore Tilton to a pretty, dark-eyed young woman named Elizabeth Richards who like her husband regarded Beecher with adoration. *The Independent* became one of America's most widely read newspapers, largely due to Beecher's regular contribution, "The Star Papers". It was partly through the influence of Theodore Tilton that Beecher preached liberal doctrines.

In 1862, the attractive and popular Lucy Bowen died at the age of thirty-eight; she had borne ten children. On her death bed she beckoned her husband to move closer and whispered into his ear a confession that stunned him. She had been committing adultery with Henry Ward Beecher. Henry Bowen was in a difficult position. He was convulsed by jealousy and resentment: the man he had brought from Indiana and made editor of his newspaper had been his wife's lover. Beecher's column ceased to appear in *The Independent* and not long after Beecher himself left for England to preach the doctrines of anti-slavery. It was many years before he and Bowen renewed their friendship. When Beecher returned from England, Tilton insisted that he should become a regular visitor at his house; he wanted to share his friend with his wife. If anyone had told him that this would one day involve *sharing* his wife with his friend, he would have been furiously indignant; no one believed more deeply than Tilton in Beecher's total honesty and integrity.

Theodore Tilton, like Henry Ward Beecher, had started life as a highly orthodox young man who would "rather have had my right hand cut off than have written a letter on the Sabbath." Yet when he had met the seventeen-year-old Elizabeth Richards — known to all as Libby — their passion had been so intense that they consummated their love before Beecher joined them in wedlock. Ten years after their marriage, Tilton began to experience "doubts" — about Christ's divinity, the absolute authority of the Bible, and other such weighty matters. Libby was horrified and Beecher had to comfort and soothe her. While her husband was away lecturing, Libby wrote him long letters in which she spoke freely of her love for Beecher. Neither she nor her

Rev. Henry Ward Beecher

husband experienced any misgivings; both believed implicitly that the highest form of love is wholly spiritual, and that such love casts out carnal desire. So Libby went on playing with fire, assuring herself that she was part of a "blessed trinity" rather than an eternal triangle. In 1867, Beecher signed a contract to write a novel for which he was to receive the record sum of $24,000. (His sister was Harriet Beecher Stowe, author of *Uncle Tom's Cabin*.) He would bring the novel — *Norwood* — to Libby's house to ask her advice.

In August 1868, the Tiltons' baby son, Paul, died of cholera. Soon afterwards, Theodore Tilton set out on another of his lecture trips. On 9 October Libby went to hear Beecher deliver a speech at the Brooklyn Academy of Music and was overwhelmed with admiration. On the following day, Libby called on him at his home. That afternoon the inevitable happened: Libby became his mistress. It seems to have been Beecher who took the lead, since she later explained that she had "yielded to him" in gratitude for the sympathy he gave her on the death of her child. Beecher had apparently assured her that their love was divine and that having sexual intercourse was its proper and valid expression, like a handshake or a kiss. He insisted that she should guard their secret — he called it "nest hiding", borrowing the terminology from bird-watching. Not long after this, Beecher called on Libby at her home at 174 Livingston Street in Brooklyn, and once again they made love. After that, they made love on a number of occasions, at their respective homes, and in "various other places".

But the delicate, romantic Libby was not made for adultery. It began to prey on her mind. Beecher enjoyed sex much more than she did and wanted to make love every time they were alone. He obviously enjoyed it so much that Libby began to wonder whether it could be true that their relationship was blessed by God. In the summer of 1870,

Scandals

Libby went to pass the hot months – as was her custom – at Schoharie, New York. But on 3 July tormented by conscience, she returned to Brooklyn and confessed everything to her husband.

Tilton was deeply shaken. His initial reaction, understandably, was to denounce the "whited sepulchre", but his wife had preceded her confession with the demand that he would not harm the person implicated. His mind was still in confusion the next day when he went to his office. He admitted later that his chief desire was to find some excuse for his wife. He decided that ". . . she sinned as one in a trance. I don't think she was a free agent. I think she would have done his bidding if, like the heathen-priest in the Hindoo-land, he had bade her fling her child into the Ganges . . ." In this he showed a great deal of insight – there can be no doubt that Libby Tilton regarded herself as Beecher's slave, to do with as he would. Tilton then decided that he would not denounce Beecher, but that his punishment would be that Libby herself would go and tell him that she had confessed to her husband. Having decided "in my secret self to be a conqueror", Tilton experienced a kind of ecstasy; for the next two weeks, "I walked the streets as if I scarcely touched the ground." Then human nature asserted itself. He had to tell somebody. One evening three prominent figures in the feminist movement came to the house and Tilton unburdened himself about the "lecherous scoundrel who has defiled my bed". When he came back from seeing two of the ladies home, the third – a woman named Sue Anthony – had to interpose herself between Tilton and his wife as he railed at her. She was later to allege that Libby Tilton then confessed in detail to her adultery with Beecher.

Libby then made the immense mistake of telling her mother – a psychotic and an impossible lady named Mrs Nathan B. Morse – about her affair. Mrs Morse had separated from her second husband after trying to strangle him to death. She hated Tilton and adored Beecher. Now she glimpsed the marvellous possibility that Libby might divorce Tilton and marry Beecher; she set about promoting this end by gossiping all over Brooklyn about the scandal, writing abusive letters to her son-in-law, and insinuating letters to Beecher that began "My dear son . . ."

On Christmas Eve that year, Libby Tilton suffered a miscarriage; she later referred to it as "a love babe" and there seems no doubt that she believed the child to be Beecher's. She was in a state of agonized misery. Her husband hardly ever spoke to her — he spent much of his time at the house of a friend called Frank Moulton, who became his confidant — and on one occasion, she went to the graveyard and lay down on the grave of her two dead children until a keeper made her move on.

Mrs Morse's gossip finally reached the ears of Henry Bowen, the other man Beecher had cuckolded. He immediately saw it as a marvellous opportunity to get his own back on Beecher without compromising the reputation of his dead wife (he had now remarried). Bowen asked Tilton to go and see him and then proceeded to accuse Beecher of being an inveterate seducer. According to Bowen, Beecher was even a rapist — he had thrown down a well-known authoress on the sofa and taken her by force. The story of Beecher's seduction of the former Mrs Bowen was repeated. Finally, Tilton was persuaded to write a letter to Beecher, ordering him to renounce his ministry and quit Brooklyn "for reasons he well understood". Bowen promised to deliver this. But Bowen was playing a double game. He was too much of a coward to want to confront Beecher openly. What he wanted to do was to pretend he was the friend of both parties, while setting them at one another's throats. He went to Beecher, gave him the letter, then assured him that he was on his side and that Tilton was himself a seducer of many women. (This seems to be true — Tilton apparently admitted to one of Bowen's employees,

Scandals

Oliver Johnson, that he had even slept with one of his mistresses in his own home.) Meanwhile, Tilton decided to use Frank Moulton as a go-between; he made his wife write a confession of her adultery, then sent Moulton to tell Beecher about it. This was the first Beecher knew about Libby's confession of adultery.

Beecher now went to see Libby, who was still in bed after her miscarriage. And he succeeded in persuading her to write a letter in which she declared that her confession had been untrue, wrung out of her by her husband's jealousy. There followed more to-ing and fro-ing between the various parties which ended finally in an uneasy truce between Beecher and the wronged husband. Beecher heaved a sigh of relief; it looked as if his sins would not find him out after all.

But he had reckoned without an extraordinary lady named Victoria Woodhull, an ardent "women's libber" of the period, who became known as "Mrs Satan" because she preached the doctrine of "free love". Victoria Woodhull was, in her way, as remarkable a character as Beecher himself. She was the daughter of a riverboat gambler and maidservant, and as a child she discovered she was psychic. She became a clairvoyant and spirit medium. At fifteen she married an alcoholic doctor named Woodhull, to whom she bore a child. She divorced him when she met a spiritualist named Colonel Blood but allowed Woodhull to continue living in the household. Then she made her greatest conquest: she and her equally remarkable sister Tennessee Claflin persuaded one of America's richest men, old Commodore Vanderbilt, that they could heal his various ailments with "magnetism". Vanderbilt fell in love with Tennessee (or Tennie C, as Victoria's younger sister preferred to spell it). He set them up in a brokerage business and financed a magazine called *Woodhull and Claflin's Weekly*, in which Victoria preached her doctrines of free love, attacked the rich (though not, of course, Vanderbilt) and espoused Marxism.

On 22 May 1871, Victoria published in the *World* a letter in which she praised free love "in its highest, purest sense as the only cure for immorality", and stated that people who attacked her were hypocrites. "I know of one man, a public teacher of eminence, who lives in concubinage with the wife of another public teacher." And she sent Theodore Tilton a message asking him to come and see her. Tilton had by now been sacked by Bowen, but with the help of Beecher, had started another magazine called *The Golden Age*. He was curious to see the notorious "free lover" and hurried round to her office. He found her to be a highly attractive woman in her early thirties who seemed far less formidable than he expected — even when she showed him her letter in the newspaper. Soon he and Victoria became good friends — in fact, Victoria was later to declare that they became lovers. Tilton no doubt told himself that he was only trying to prevent a scandal by keeping Victoria friendly. Victoria Woodhull also met Beecher and admitted that she found him a magnetic and attractive personality. But when Beecher declined to introduce Victoria at a suffragette meeting (where he knew she was going to preach free love), Tilton stepped into the gap. It did his reputation no good at all to be publicly associated with "Mrs Satan" and her scandalous doctrines. Unfortunately, Victoria was so carried away by her new popularity with the women's movement (which had formerly regarded her as a crank), that she allowed herself to denounce her former protector Commodore Vanderbilt as a capitalist; he promptly dropped her. In May 1872, Victoria announced that she was standing as the first woman president of the United States, with a Negro reform leader as her running mate. She was infuriated when Tilton declined to support her cause and instead declared his support for Horace Greeley. (Because of the bad reputation he was acquiring, Tilton's support did Greeley no good at all.) Victoria Woodhull became increasingly angry and embittered. And finally she did what Beecher had always feared she would do: she told the whole story of his affair with Libby Tilton and the subsequent "cover up", in her magazine. The result was as sensational as she had hoped. The magazine sold 100,000 copies and could have sold many times that number — copies began to change hands for as much as $40. A young man named Anthony Comstock, the vice warden for the Young Men's Christian Association, saw the story, was outraged at this smear on the saintly Henry Ward Beecher, and was responsible for the arrest of the Claflin sisters for sending indecent material through the United States mails. Victoria and Tennessee went to jail. But the damage was done. The whole country was now gossiping about the Beecher-Tilton scandal. Six months later, when Victoria and her sister were acquitted (on the grounds that their accusations did not constitute pornography), everyone in the country wanted to know whether Tilton was a cuckold and Beecher was a seducer.

Beecher's own congregation increased his problems by insisting on expelling Tilton from the church. If, as Beecher insisted, he was innocent of adultery, then Tilton was a wicked traducer. Tilton, who had so far been more-or-less on Beecher's side (at least in wanting to suppress the scandal) now began to smoulder with resentment. This was not assuaged when Beecher decided to air the scandal by holding a "trial" in his own church and Libby was persuaded to leave her husband and take Beecher's side. The church committee, predictably, decided that Beecher was not guilty. Tilton was branded as a liar. On 24 August 1874, Tilton swore out a complaint against Beecher, charging him with having wilfully alienated his wife's affections.

The Beecher-Tilton trial began on 11 January 1875, and lasted until 2 July. The whole nation was agog. Beecher spent much of his time in court; so did his sour-faced wife Eunice (known locally as "the Griffin"). Beecher took the line that he had never, at any time, sinned with Libby Tilton, but that he fully acknowledged his guilt in having allowed her to idolize him to the exclusion of her husband — this, he claimed, was the meaning of some of the letters he had written admitting his guilt.

During those six months, the American public had more than its fill of scandal. It learned that Beecher was accused of seducing Lucy Bowen as well as Libby Tilton. One newspaper cartoon showed a Brooklyn businessman locking his wife in a huge safe with a notice on the door, Proof Against Fire And Clergymen, while another showed a hatter who sold the "new style of Brooklyn hat" — with horns on it. The public also learned that the wronged husband was not entirely innocent. He was alleged to have seduced the seventeen-year-old daughter of a congressman named Lovejoy in Winsted, Connecticut, and to have made an unsuccessful attempt to seduce a young girl who formed part of his household; this girl, Elizabeth Turner, told how Tilton had laid on her bed, kissed her, and put his hand "down her neck" (i.e. on her breast). On another occasion he had come into her bedroom when she was fast asleep and carried her out; if he had failed to seduce her, it was plainly not for want of trying. The story of Tilton's "affair" with

---

The philosopher A.J. Ayer was a notorious seducer. One of his mistresses, the stage designer Jocelyn Rickard, records in her autobiography *The Painted Banquet* that she broke off her affair with him when he had acquired seven more mistresses — not because she was jealous, but because there were not enough nights in the week.

Scandals

Victoria Woodhull was also raked up. On the other hand, various servants testified to having seen Beecher in situations of intimacy with Libby Tilton; even her own brother reluctantly admitted that he had walked into the room and seen Beecher and Libby separating with obvious embarrassment. Libby herself, like Beecher, denied any misconduct.

The jury was out for eight days; it was unable to reach a unanimous verdict but voted nine to three against Tilton. Beecher's supporters regarded this as a triumph and he left the court like a conquering hero. His trials were not quite over, however. Frank Moulton sued Beecher for malicious prosecution but the suit was dismissed. Then Henry Bowen demanded that the Plymouth Church Committee should try Beecher for adultery with Lucy Bowen. The Committee disbelieved him and Bowen, like the Moultons, was expelled from the church. Beecher made a lecture tour of the country and although he was booed in many places, he never failed to draw enormous crowds. When he died, thirteen years later (in 1887) his popularity with his own congregation was as great as ever.

Theodore Tilton also continued to lecture but his fortunes declined. He left the country in 1883, to settle finally in Paris, where he wrote novels and romantic poetry, and spent his days in a café playing chess. Libby, deserted by her husband and her lover, became a schoolteacher; she remains the most pathetic figure in the case. The Woodhull sisters both married rich men, and Victoria died in 1927, at the age of eighty-nine.

In retrospect, it is difficult not to agree with the reporter who wrote: "Mankind fell in Adam and has been falling ever since, but never touched bottom until it got to Henry Ward Beecher."

John Hugh Smyth Pigott –
The "Abode of Love" Scandal

The Reverend John Hugh Smyth Pigott threw his congregation into noisy disarray when he announced, during a Sunday evening service in 1902, that he was the Lord Jesus Christ arisen. The several hundred worshippers, gathered in the Agapemonite 'Ark of the Covenant' church in Clapton, North London, did not react as orthodox Christians might have expected. Not a soul dissented; instead the whole congregation fell to their knees weeping and praising the Lord who stood before them.

The Agapemonites believed with absolute certainty that they were living in the last days before the Final Judgement and many had fostered the hope that their leader might be the Lord of Hosts. For the fifty-six years since it's founding, the Church of the Agapemone, meaning 'Abode of Love', had caused controversy, but never as much as it did that day in Clapton. So, while the Reverend Pigott's disciples rejoiced, their enemies delighted in what they saw as the Agapemonites' greatest folly and, they hoped, their ultimate downfall.

The sect was founded in 1846 by a thirty-five-year-old renegade Church of England curate, Henry James Prince. It began as a small religious commune of divinity students at the village of Spaxton, near Bridgewater in Somerset. The community, housed in a single large building, was named Agapemone by its founder and gave its name to the the developing sect.

Reverend Prince built the 'Abode of Love' with a sizable legacy he had received from his wife and from the start the community prospered both spiritually and financially. All the adherents and their loved ones lived together at the Abode, gladly sharing all their worldly possessions under the eyes of the Lord, as they called Reverend Prince.

Outsiders soon noted that there were significantly more

25

women than men in the commune and it soon got about that Reverend Prince encouraged free love. Lawsuits pressed by the families of several of the unmarried women who had joined the community, successfully regained some of the money taken into the community coffers and a Chancery Court in 1860 noted that 'breaches of decorum and manners' had taken place at Agapemone.

Yet, despite the antagonism, the Agapemonites prospered and grew. The donation of all worldly goods made by fresh converts enabled the members of the sect to live quite comfortably and ensured that they were never short of cash. When a wealthy London businessman joined the faith he gladly pooled his entire fortune with the rest; as a sign of special favour "the Lord" made him his personal butler.

Prince was convinced that the Second Coming was at hand and saw himself as the new John the Baptist. He did not however, adopt the original Baptist's spartan way of life, preferring to live more like a rich aristocrat. For example, he travelled widely at home and abroad in a magnificent coach-and-six with liveried outriders and a pack of hounds always at hand. Since they were living well themselves, his followers did not begrudge him his little pleasures, keeping in mind his words: 'The time of prayer is past and the time of grace has come.'

In 1896, fifty years after the founding of the sect, the eighty-five-year-old Reverend Prince decided that expansion was in order. With commune money he commissioned the building of an impressively large church with an attached mansion, in the London Borough of Clapton. He named the church the 'Ark of the Covenant', and had the words 'Love in Judgement and Judgement unto Victory' inscribed over the entrance. The new church attracted many people to join the sect and it seemed the Agapemonites had reached a new pinnacle.

Unfortunately, a major blow came just three years later.

Prince, as the new John the Baptist was considered literally immortal by both his followers and himself; it seemed inconceivable that he should die before the Final Judgement, after which the chosen would live for ever. His death at the age of eighty-eight deeply shook his followers.

Into the spiritual breach stepped the Reverend John Hugh Smyth Pigott, a Church of England curate like Prince and the Lord's favoured disciple. At fifty-years-old Reverend Pigott was an imposing man, tall and lean with intense eyes and a resounding voice. Under his new leadership the Agapemonites overcame the loss of the Lord and continued to prosper.

Then three years later, in 1902, Reverend Pigott announced his assumption of Godhead. His faithful flock took this in their stride − for decades they had lived with a benign leader to whom they had ascribed virtual deification and this simply seemed the next step towards Judgement Day − but other Londoners were less enthusiastic. A large crowd gathered to view the new Messiah the following Sunday, very few of them friendly.

As Pigott and his retinue arrived for the evening service the police had to hold the angry mob back. When he entered the Ark of the Covenant many of the crowd managed to climb the iron railings surrounding the church grounds and thronged the pews. Pigott's sermon was drowned-out by their cat-calls and as he left he had to dodge a shower of stones and bricks hurled by indignant unbelievers. One local paper noted that, "this self-styled Messiah would probably have been thrown into the pond at Clapton Common but for the protection of the mounted police."

In the face of this unchristian behaviour Pigott retired with his wife Kathie and disciples to the Abode of Love in Somerset. Once there he clearly decided to refrain from making any more public claims to divinity and the local people seemed glad to leave the sect in peace. Reverend

Pigott settled down to a quieter life with his family which now included his "spiritual bride", Ruth Preece.

At this time the Church of England still considered him to be a member of the Anglican clergy, as did Pigott himself. That he had claimed to be Christ the Redeemer did not stir his bishop to action, but the fact that he subsequently begot two boys, whom he called Power and Glory, with a merely "spiritual bride", brought-about an immediate charge of immoral behaviour from the Bishop of Bath-and-Wells. Pigott was defrocked on the floor of Wells Cathedral in 1909.

This, of course, had no effect on his standing as a spiritual leader with the Agapemonites, but their numbers were now on the wane. At the time of his defrocking the movement consisted of only about a hundred women and a handful of men, but despite the hopes of their enemies the Agapemonites soldiered on. Pigott died in 1927, at the age of seventy-eight, leaving only a few followers.

His spiritual bride, Sister Ruth, who had borne him another child, carried on the faith until her death in 1956. The old woman was mourned by the fifteen remaining members of the Agapemonite church. Shortly thereafter another fringe sect took over the Ark of the Covenant church in Clapton and the Abode of Love was sold and converted into council flats.

Fatty Arbuckle – A Star's Disgrace

The scandal that wrecked the career of film comic 'Fatty' Roscoe Arbuckle – and tarnished the image of Hollywood – occurred after a three-day drinking party in 1921.

Arbuckle was born on 24 March 1887 in Smith Center, Kansas, USA and named Roscoe Conklin Arbuckle. He worked as a plumber's assistant, then became a performer in carnivals and vaudeville – for all his enormous weight (303 lb or 21 stone) he was incredibly agile. At the age of twenty-one he was hired as an extra by the Selig Polyscope Company and he made his first one-reel comedy – *The Sanitarium* – in 1910. He was hired by Mack Sennett and made a dozen films in 1913 including *Fatty's Day Off* and *Fatty's Flirtation*. His attraction lay in his cherubic innocence – the good nature that he radiated was obviously genuine. Neither, for a Hollywood star, was he unusually sex-oriented; the girls he worked with found him protective and "big brotherly". His reputation was a great deal better, for example, than that of his co-star Charlie Chaplin. In 1917, he moved with Sennett to Jesse Lasky's Artcraft, and wrote and directed most of his own films. He gave Buster Keaton a start in life. When he made a film for Paramount, a banner over the gate read: Welcome To The Prince Of Whales. But an all-night party laid on in his honour by Jesse Lasky in Boston on 6 March in 1917, almost led to scandal. Twelve party girls were paid over $1,000 for their night's work. But some Boston resident who peered through the transom and saw Fatty stripping on a table with several girls called the police. It is alleged that Lasky, Adolph Zukor and Joseph Schenck ended by paying the district attorney and mayor $10,000 to overlook the incident.

In 1921, Arbuckle signed a contract worth $3 million and he decided to celebrate with a party in the St Francis Hotel in San Francisco. He arrived from Bay City on the evening of Saturday, 3 September 1921, and took a suite, as well as three rooms on the twelfth floor, in the unlikely event that anyone should want to sleep. By the following afternoon, the party was in full swing, with about fifty guests, including such Hollywood cronies as Lowell Sherman and Freddy Fishback, and a number of pretty actresses. Arbuckle, separated from his wife, had asked his friend Bambina Maude Delmont to invite a girl he particularly admired – the starlet Virginia Rappe. The two women were staying at the nearby Palace Hotel, together with Virginia's agent.

Fatty Arbuckle with Virginia Rappe, the girl he was accused of raping

Twenty-five-year-old Virginia Rappe was a model from Chicago, who had achieved public notice when her face appeared on the sheet music of "Let Me Call You Sweetheart". She was a pretty, fresh-faced girl, the type Hollywood liked to cast as a milkmaid – dressed in a check frock and sunbonnet she looked the essence of female innocence. According to film-maker Kenneth Anger (in *Hollywood Babylon*) this appearance was misleading. "An offer came from Sennett, and she went to work on his lot, taking minor parts. She also did her share of sleeping around, and gave half the company crabs. This epidemic so shocked Sennett that he closed down his studio and had it fumigated." Arbuckle had been pursuing Virginia – without success – for five years. She found him unattractive and was later quoted as having said: "I'd sooner go to bed with a jungle ape than have that fat octopus groping at me." But since Arbuckle was now an influential figure in the film world and Virginia was still an unknown starlet, she was willing to make certain compromises to advance her career.

On Labour Day, Monday, 5 September 1921, the party was still going, and Virginia had come from the Palace Hotel, accompanied by a "bodyguard". Arbuckle was still dressed in pyjamas, carpet slippers and a bathrobe. Most of the other guests were in a similar state of *déshabillé*. Virginia refused champagne and accepted a gin and orange. She was drinking her third – and was anxious to get to the bathroom, which seemed to be constantly occupied – when Arbuckle grabbed her and steered her into a bedroom, winking at his friends and commenting: "This is what I've been waiting for."

A few minutes later, there were screams from the bedroom. Suddenly, the party noises died away. Maude Delmont went and tried the bedroom handle, calling, "Virginia, what's happening?" There were more screams. Maude Delmont picked up the telephone and called down for the manager. The assistant manager, H.J. Boyle, rushed into the suite just as the door of bedroom 1219 burst open and Arbuckle appeared with Virginia's hat perched on his head at an absurd angle. He gave an innocent smile and did a little dance on the carpet. Back in the room, Virginia was making groaning sounds. Fatty's good temper seemed to slip and he said to Maude Delmont, "Get her dressed and take her back to the Palace." And when Virginia started to scream again he yelled, "Shut up, or I'll throw you out of the window."

Virginia was lying on the bed, almost nude, with her clothes scattered around her. She was moaning, "I'm dying, I'm dying. He hurt me." They tried to dress her, but her blouse was badly torn – it had obviously been ripped from her by force.

The house doctor was sent for and Virginia was moved to another room, still moaning. Arbuckle seemed to feel she was "putting it on", perhaps to blackmail him into offering her a part, and snapped, "Shut up. You were always a lousy actress."

She was in pain for the next three days, often becoming unconscious. She was transferred to a nursing home, where she died. The doctor who performed the autopsy discovered that her bladder was ruptured. The result was death from peritonitis. What had happened seemed clear. Arbuckle had flung himself on her with his full weight when she had a full bladder and it had ruptured like a balloon. When it was reported to the coroner, police interviewed hospital staff to find out who was behind the accident. The next morning newspaper headlines all over the country talked about the orgy that had ended in rape and death.

An inquest found that Arbuckle was "criminally responsible" for Virginia's death and recommended that he should be charged with manslaughter. Even before he went on trial in November, his career was in ruins. The fat, innocent man who made everybody laugh was really a "sex fiend". Rumours had it that his penis was so enormous that it had ruptured her bladder. But Arbuckle's friend Al Semi-nacher introduced a note of horror when he told people that Arbuckle had used a large piece of ice from the ice bucket to penetrate Virginia. Rumour added that he had first assaulted her by introducing a champagne bottle.

Church groups and women's clubs demanded that his films should be withdrawn from circulation, and that unreleased films should never be shown. It was hardly necessary. No one could laugh at Arbuckle when they remembered that this innocent, babylike character had torn off a girl's clothes and raped her. A "Fatty lynching" mood swept the country: in Wyoming, cowboys shot up the screen of a cinema showing an Arbuckle short; in Hartford, Connecticut, women tore down the screen.

Arbuckle was released on bail. His trial began in November; he denied doing any harm to Virginia and his lawyers did their best to suggest that she was little better than a prostitute. After forty-three hours deliberation, a jury was in favour of acquitting Arbuckle by ten to two, but a majority verdict was not good enough and a mistrial was declared. At his second trial, the jury found him guilty by ten to two and again they were dismissed. On 12 April 1922, a third jury found him innocent, and the foreman added: "Acquittal is not enough. We feel a grave injustice has been done him and there is not the slightest proof to connect him in any way with the commission of a crime." Outside the court, Arbuckle told newsmen, "My innocence of the hideous charge preferred against me has been proved." But it made no difference. Comedy depends upon a make-believe world in which no one does any real harm and everything is a joke. Fatty's "rape" had introduced a brutal element of reality. This was the real reason why he remained unforgiven.

The $3 million contract was cancelled and his unreleased films were suppressed. It cost the studio $1 million. His friend Buster Keaton suggested he should change his name to Will B. Good. In fact, he directed a few comedy shorts under the name of William Goodrich. He toured America's backwoods in second-rate farces, but some of them were booed off the stage. In 1931 he pleaded in *Photoplay*: "Just let me work . . . I think I can entertain and gladden the people that see me." He seemed incapable of grasping that the case had somehow undermined the public's willingness to laugh at him.

He began to drink heavily: in 1931 he was arrested in Hollywood for drunken driving. Yet in 1933, his luck seemed to be turning. Warner Brothers took the risk of hiring him to make several short comedies. But after a celebration party in a New York hotel on 28 June 1933, he returned to his room and died of a heart attack. He was forty-six years old.

Towards the end of his life, the French novelist Henri Murger, author of *La Bohéme*, was seen standing in a urinal, groping inside his trousers and muttering: "Come on out, you little devil. It's only to pee."

Chapter Two

Financial Scandals

B *ribery is a dirty word and when it involves policemen it becomes even dirtier. In 1877 Scotland Yard was at the centre of a large cover-up scandal that involved several high-ranking policemen. And even to this day, people will often offer a bribe to get out of a sticky situation that is of their own making.*

Scotland Yard – The Great Bribery Scandal

Harry Benson, one of the most ingenious swindlers of all time, is remembered chiefly for his leading role in the great Scotland Yard scandal of 1877.

Benson was the son of a well-to-do Jewish merchant with offices in the Faubourg St Honoré in Paris. He had charming manners, spoke several languages, and liked to represent himself as a member of the nobility. Soon after the Franco-Prussian war of 1870–71, he approached the Lord Mayor of London, calling himself the Comte de Montague, Mayor of Châteaudun, seeking a subscription for the relief of citizens made destitute by the war. He collected £1,000 but his forged receipt gave him away and he was sentenced to a year in prison. He found prison life so intolerable that he attempted suicide by trying to burn himself to death on his prison mattress. He was crippled by it and had to walk with crutches thereafter.

When he came out of prison, Benson advertised for a secretarial position, mentioning that he spoke several languages. The man who answered his advertisement

Scandals

was a certain William Kurr, who specialized in swindles connected with racing. His crude method was to decamp hastily with his customers' winnings. The ingenious Benson soon convinced him that there were better and less risky ways of making a fortune. Members of the French aristocracy were the chosen victims. Kurr and Benson issued a newspaper called *Le Sport* which contained articles about racing translated from British newspapers. It also contained many references to a wealthy Mr G. H. Yonge, who was so incredibly successful in backing horses that British bookmakers always shortened their odds when they dealt with him. *Le Sport* was sent out, free, to dozens of French aristocrats interested in racing; they had no earthly reason for suspecting a prospective swindle.

One of the aristocrats who became a victim was a certain Comtesse de Goncourt. She received a letter from Mr Yonge of Shanklin, Isle of Wight, asking her if she would agree to act as his agent in laying bets. All she had to do was to send the cheque he would send her to a certain bookmaker; if the horse won, she would receive his winnings, which she would forward to Mr Yonge, and would receive a 5 per cent commission. Madame de Goncourt agreed to this arrangement and received a cheque for a few hundred pounds, which she posted off to the bookmaker in her own name. In due course, she received a cheque for more than a thousand pounds in "winnings" and after she had sent this off to Mr Yonge, she received her £50 or so commission. It seemed a marvellously easy way of earning £50. What she did not realize was that the "bookmaker" to whom she forwarded the cheque was simply another of Mr Yonge's aliases. When she had sent Mr Yonge several more lots of winnings and received several more lots of commission, she decided that he was obviously a financial genius and entrusted him with £10,000 of her own money to invest on her behalf. That was the last she saw of it.

Although Scotland Yard was a relatively new institution in the 1870s (it was established in 1829), its methods of crime-fighting depended a great deal on underworld "narks" who betrayed fellow criminals. Police officers, then as now, were forced to cultivate the acquaintance of many criminals. It also meant that an underpaid police officer – in those days the salary of a detective was a mere £5 6s. 2d. a week – might be subjected to the temptation of accepting presents, favours and open bribes for protecting his own "narks". This may well be how a certain detective officer named John Meiklejohn became friendly with William Kurr and then began to accept money from him in exchange for not pressing his investigations into Kurr's earlier swindles. When Chief Inspector Nathaniel Druscovich, a naturalized Pole, confided to Chief Inspector Meiklejohn that he was in financial difficulties, Meiklejohn told him he knew a "businessman" who could help him. The businessman was Benson and all he wanted in return for the £60 he "lent" Druscovich was a little information – prior warning if the Yard intended to arrest him. Soon a third detective had been drawn into the net – Chief Inspector William Palmer. Not long after this, Meiklejohn warned Kurr and Benson that the Yard was getting close. Meiklejohn's superior, Chief Inspector Clarke, had been tracking down sham betting offices and was hot on the trail of Gardner and Co., the name under which Kurr and his confederates had been operating.

Among these confederates was a man called Walters who belonged to a gang that Clarke had recently broken up. Now Benson wrote to Clarke from his pleasant home in the Isle of Wight – he kept a carriage, and had an excellent cook and many servants – saying that he had some interesting information about Walters. Unfortunately, he explained, he was crippled and could not come to Scotland Yard but if Clarke would be kind enough to come down to Shanklin . . . In those days, policemen stood in awe of the aristocracy and were likely to treat a wealthy suspect with obsequious respect. So Clarke hurried down to Shanklin and was duly overawed by Mr Yonge's magnificent home. He was worried when Mr Yonge told him that Walters was going about saying that he had bribed Clarke and that he had in his possession a letter to prove it. Indeed Clarke had written Walters a letter; he was not a very literate man and he might easily have expressed himself in a way that could be open to false interpretation. Mr Yonge promised to try to get hold of the letter and he and Clarke parted on friendly terms. But Clarke then reported to his own superior that Yonge was a scoundrel. They had some correspondence and Yonge addressed Clarke as "My Dear Sir and Brother" for they were both freemasons. They met several times and "Yonge" later claimed he had given Clarke £50.

With this network of "police spies", the Benson-Kurr gang should have been untouchable. But Benson now overstepped himself. He wrote to the Comtesse de Goncourt saying that he had a marvellous and unique opportunity to invest a further large sum for her. The Comtesse had no more ready cash and she called on her lawyer, a Mr Abrahams, to ask him to turn certain securities into cash. Mr Abrahams took the precaution of contacting Scotland Yard and asking whether they knew anything about a certain Mr Yonge of "Rose Bank", Shanklin. Druscovich, who was in charge of frauds connected with the Continent, received the message and hastened to warn Benson that trouble was brewing. Scotland Yard had been asked by the Paris police to intercept letters containing money from various dupes – but the telegram containing this request was pocketed by Druscovich. Druscovich could see that he was playing a dangerous game; he would be expected to make an arrest soon. He begged the swindlers to remove themselves beyond his reach as soon as possible.

Briton William George Stern was a tycoon with the dubious honour of holding a world record for the largest bankruptcy — he lost £104,390,248. Stern, however, was one step ahead of his creditors and had placed his house, his paintings and his Rolls-Royce under the ownership of his family trust, placing them out of their reach. The former millionaire agreed to pay £6,000 a year to settle his debts, which would leave some of his creditors waiting seventeen thousand years to be paid off.

The gang, which included Kurr's brother Frederick, and two men named Murray and Bale, had put most of its ill-gotten gains into the safest place, the Bank of England. They could, of course, withdraw it without difficulty. The only problem about that was that English bank notes are numbered and for such a large sum of money, they would be numbered consecutively and would, therefore, be easy to trace. If the gang escaped to the Continent, they would be leaving a trail of bank notes behind them like a paperchase. Benson withdrew about £16,000 from the bank and hastened up to Scotland where he opened an account in the Bank of Clydesdale in Greenock; he also withdrew £13,000 in Bank of Clydesdale £100 notes. These had the advantage of bearing no number but they were still easily traceable. Benson was eating dinner with the manager of the Clydesdale Bank when he received a telegram from Druscovich warning him that he was on his way to arrest him. Benson fled, forfeiting the £3,000 still in his account at Greenock.

The detectives were rewarded with about £500 each

(although Clarke does not seem to have been included). Meiklejohn immediately made the mistake of cashing one of his £100 notes and giving an office of the gang as his address. A week later he cashed another note with a Leeds wine merchant. The Leeds Police discovered this and, since they were on the lookout for the gang, sent a telegram to Scotland Yard. Druscovich intercepted the telegram and burned it.

Scotland Yard found it baffling that, in spite of all their efforts, the Benson gang had slipped through their fingers. The bribed detectives were still not suspected. Clarke's superior, Williamson set it all down to sheer bad luck. In fact, most of the gang was now in hiding at Bridge of Allan in Scotland. When the Comtesse's lawyer Abrahams traced them to Scotland, Detective Officer William Palmer sent them a letter warning them to scatter.

It was Druscovich who was made responsible for rushing around the country to trap the swindlers. He met Kurr at the Caledonian Station in Edinburgh and was offered £1,000 by him if he did not go to Bridge of Allan. Druscovich had to decline for he had been ordered to go to Bridge of Allan to collect certain letters that had been addressed to one "Mr Giffard" at the Queen's Hotel. Mr Giffard was William Kurr.

Inevitably, the birds had flown by the time Druscovich reached Bridge of Allan. Williamson was understandably disappointed. He was astounded to learn that his subordinate, Meiklejohn had been seen in the company of the swindlers at Bridge of Allan. This was surely the point when Scotland Yard had to smell a rat . . . But Meiklejohn explained that he had no idea he had been wining and dining with crooks. He had met Yonge by chance and believed him to be a perfectly respectable gentleman. Williamson accepted his story.

Now the gang found themselves with thousands of pounds in uncashable £100 notes and with no ready cash. Murray was sent off to cash a cheque at one of the banks in Scotland where they had opened an account; the police were waiting for him. Benson went to Rotterdam and tried to cash a note at his hotel but Scotland Yard had alerted the Dutch police and he was arrested. Druscovich passed on the news to Kurr who persuaded a crooked attorney named Froggatt to send the Dutch police a telegram signed "Scotland Yard", ordering them to release Benson on the grounds that his arrest had been a mistake. It almost succeeded but the Dutch police decided to wait for a letter confirming the telegram, and this never came.

It was Druscovich, the expert on Continental crime, who was sent to Rotterdam to bring back Benson – and Bale, who had also been arrested there. There was nothing he could do about it except to look at them sternly and mutter under his breath that he would do his best. There was no opportunity to allow them to escape. Besides, his own position was now in danger. Williamson had now heard about the letter from the Leeds Police, telling them that Meiklejohn had cashed a £100 note there. He wanted to know if Druscovich had seen it. Druscovich denied all knowledge of it and he realized that any attempt to allow Benson to escape was now out of the question.

The swindlers finally stood in the dock and were found guilty. Benson received fifteen years and Kurr received ten. As soon as they reached Millbank Prison, they asked to see the governor and told the story of the corrupt detectives. A short time afterwards, Druscovich, Meiklejohn, Palmer and Clarke all stood in the dock – and, for good measure, the police had also arrested the crooked attorney Froggatt. Many letters from the detectives were produced, warning the crooks of the activities of Scotland Yard. Druscovich had also been seen talking to Benson and Kurr at St Pancras Station, London.

All except Clarke were convicted – the evidence against Clarke was inconclusive. Druscovich, Meiklejohn and

Scandals

Palmer all received two years' hard labour, the maximum sentence for conspiring to defeat the ends of justice.

Clarke was retired on a pension. Meiklejohn became a private detective. Palmer used his savings to become a publican. What happened to Druscovich is not known but he disappeared from sight; while Froggatt died in a workhouse.

The two principal swindlers still had many successful years before them. Benson and Kurr both received a remission of sentence for good conduct. They teamed up again and slipped across the Atlantic where they became mining company promoters. Benson returned to Belgium and continued in business selling stock in non-existent mines. The Belgian Police found out more about him from Scotland Yard and arrested him. Huge quantities of postal orders and cheques, apparently sent to him by gullible

One of the greatest financial scandals in history was the notorious "South Sea Bubble", a scheme thought up by novelist Daniel Defoe and launched by Robert Harley, the Earl of Oxford, in 1720. The idea was to import African slaves to work plantations in South America. But the shares sold so well that this part of the plan was never put into operation – no one then understood the idea of "credit". After taking 8½ million pounds, confidence began to flag, shareholders began to sell, and the company collapsed. Thousands were ruined and scores committed suicide. The company's directors were heavily fined. The scandal put the Whig Opposition in power for the next four decades.

investors were found in his lodgings. He spent another two years in jail then moved to Switzerland. There he again set out to give the impression he was a wealthy stockbroker. He met a girl in his hotel, whose father was a retired general and surgeon of the Indian army. He persuaded the girl to marry him and induced the father to sell his shares and hand over the proceeds of £7,000 for "investment". Then he tried to disappear to America. His father-in-law managed to have him arrested at Bremen but decided not to prosecute when Benson gave back £5,000. Jewellery that Benson had given his fiancée proved to be made of paste.

His last great coup was in America. The singer Adelina Patti was arriving in New York for a tour. Benson, calling himself Abbey, bribed Customs officials to let him on the boat ahead of the Patti Reception Committee. He introduced himself to her as the head of the committee. When the committee arrived, he was deep in conversation with her and they assumed he was her manager. She left the boat on his arm. He then went to Mexico and sold thousands of bogus tickets of Patti concerts. He was arrested when he went back into the States and committed to the Tombs. Apparently, unable to face the prospect of another long period in prison, he leapt from a high gallery and fell 50 feet snapping his spine. At the time of his death, he was little more than forty years of age.

Teapot Dome Scandal –
The Ohio Gang Hijacks America

Warren Gamaliel Harding was probably the worst President the United States has ever had. The best that can be said of him is that the Teapot Dome scandal that erupted after his death was none of his doing; it was simply the result of his failure to do anything except play poker and make love to his mistress in a room behind the Oval office.

Scandals

Warren Harding's only asset was a ruggedly handsome face and a square jaw that made him look like a president. He was born in the small town of Corsica, Ohio, in 1865. He made half-hearted attempts to become a schoolteacher and a lawyer, and finally acquired a newspaper on the verge of bankruptcy. At about this time he met Florence Kling de Wolfe, the daughter of a leading citizen, who married him in spite of her father's bitter opposition. She was the driving force in their marriage for Harding was lazy, good natured and easy going. It was largely due to her hard work that the Marion *Star* became a successful newspaper.

As editor, Harding met many politicians, including Harry Daugherty, who lacked the personality to achieve the political ambitions he dreamed about. But Harding looked like a politician and with Daugherty as his campaign manager, he soon became a Republican State senator, then Lieutenant-Governor of Ohio. That was as far as Harding wanted to go, but his wife and Daugherty continued to push him until, to his bewilderment, he found himself elected to the United States Senate with a large majority.

Harding had no real interest in politics. He spent more time on the golf course or attending baseball games than in the Senate. He also took a mistress. A schoolgirl named Nan Britton had fallen hopelessly in love with him back in Marion and when she moved to New York they began meeting secretly. Soon she was pregnant and bore him a daughter.

In 1920, a presidential election was due; Woodrow Wilson had suffered a breakdown in 1919 and had no intention of running again. The Republicans had no clear favourite among their candidates. At the Convention in Chicago in June, none of the three main contenders was able to command a clear majority. Harding, a "dark horse", seemed an acceptable alternative. He was asked if there was any scandal in his life that might cause the party embarrassment; he emphatically denied this and was nominated on

44

the tenth ballot. In November, he beat the Democratic candidate James M. Cox and became twenty-ninth President of the United States. At the Convention, his wife had been heard to mutter, "I can see only one word written above his head if they make him President, and that word is 'Tragedy'."

It was not quite as bad as that; rather something closer to farce. Presidents do not need to be intellectual giants but Harding was barely an intellectual gnat. He was bewildered by all the tasks he ought to be tackling: post-war disarmament, world monetary problems, tariffs, tax proposals; he was like a schoolboy faced with a page of quantum equations. He invited all his cronies to the White House where they drank and played poker in his study. When Nan Britton arrived, they retired to a private room. Harding liked to sit with his waistcoat unbuttoned, his feet on the desk and a spitoon by his side, in a room thick with tobacco smoke.

Meanwhile, all his old political cronies — "the Ohio gang" — had moved to Washington and set up a kind of alternative White House on K Street. Harry Daugherty, now Attorney-General, sold government jobs and other favours, using a jobber named Jesse W. Smith as a go-between with the men who wanted to buy favours. Smith, a coarse, genial man used to love to sing: "My God, how the money rolls in."

Another member of the Ohio gang was the Secretary of the Interior, Albert Fall. Fall itched to get his hands on an enormous oil reserve known as Teapot Dome, an area of land in Wyoming, north of the town of Caspar. Woodrow Wilson had decided that Teapot Dome should be held in reserve in case of future national emergencies and it was under the control of the Naval Department. Fall persuaded the Secretary of the Navy, then the President, to transfer the lease to his Department of the Interior. Then it was secretly leased to Harry F. Sinclair, president of the

Scandals

Mammoth Oil Company, for more than $14 million. Another oil reserve at Elk Hills, California, was leased to another friend, Edward Doheny, for $100,000. Fall was soon able to pay nine years of back-taxes that he owed on a New Mexico ranch, and to stock it with prize cattle. Another Harding crony, Charles R. Forbes, was head of the Veterans' Bureau, and was in charge of purchasing supplies for hospitals for ex-servicemen and awarding contracts for new hospitals. Hospital supplies bought with public money were promptly sold as government surplus — a million towels that had cost 34 cents each were sold at 36 cents a dozen; sheets costing $1.35 a pair were sold at 27 cents a pair. Vast sums were paid to him in exchange for hospital contracts. He also received "kickbacks" from real estate dealers from whom he bought land for the hospitals at far more than its value.

Sooner or later, this empire of corruption had to collapse under its own weight. Washington journalists began to hint more and more openly at what was going on. The Attorney-General's office under Daugherty became known as the Department of Easy Virtue. Finally, the rumours reached Harding's ear. His health was breaking down — no doubt due to his intake of Bourbon — and now his nerve began to crack. A visitor to the White House took the wrong turning and was startled to come upon Harding grasping a man by the throat and shouting, "You yellow rat! You double crossing bastard!" The man was Charles Forbes, head of the Veterans' Bureau. Soon after, Forbes took a trip to Paris and sent in his resignation "for health reasons".

Jesse Smith, the go-between who liked to sing "My God, how the money rolls in", had been sent back to Ohio by Daugherty because he talked too openly. Harding summoned him to the White House and listened, aghast, as Smith told him the extent of the skulduggery. When he had finished, he asked the President what would happen now.

"Go home. Tomorrow you will be arrested." Smith went back to his hotel and shot himself.

Harding was due to make a trip to Alaska and he decided that this might be an opportune moment to escape from Washington. There was talk of a Congressional Enquiry; Charles Cramer, Forbes' right-hand man, also shot himself; there was an increasing number of resignations. As Harding returned from the Alaskan trip, down the Pacific coast, he fell ill, his doctor diagnosed food poisoning from crab meat. On 2 August 1923, he died of pneumonia. His wife died in the following year. The Teapot Dome scandal now erupted and Nan Britton added to it by writing a bestselling book about her affair with Harding called *The President's Daughter*.

When a Harding Memorial Association raised $700,000 for a monument in Marion, Ohio (where the President was buried), it was decided that it should take the form of a huge marble cylinder with colonnades. Others greatly preferred a design that was closer to a sphere. This idea was dropped when someone pointed out that it only needed a spout and a handle to look like a teapot.

Marthe Hanau was a woman after Thérèse Humbert's heart. Having built up a successful business empire, she ensured its success by creating a whole network of small journals which manipulated share prices and investments to her benefit. Fraud aside, she was a gutsy woman: when she was finally put in jail, she went on hunger strike for three weeks, escaped and then returned to prison in a taxi!

The "Suicide" of Roberto Calvi

On the morning of Friday, 18 June 1982, a postal clerk walking across Blackfriars Bridge in London looked down and saw a body dangling by its neck from the scaffolding. When the police arrived they cut down the body of a paunchy man of about sixty, with large red bricks stuffed into his pockets, and about $15,000, in various currencies, in his wallet. His passport identified him as Gian Roberto Calvini, but a check with Italian authorities revealed that he was, in fact, Roberto Calvi, chairman and managing director of the Banco Ambrosiano in Milan.

In the previous year Calvi had been sentenced to four years in prison for illegally exporting $20 million in lire; he had been released pending appeal. A week before his body was found Calvi had disappeared from his Rome apartment.

On 23 July, the London coroner decided that Calvi's death had been a suicide. By that time, however, a great deal of information about Calvi's financial associates had been unearthed, and the coroner's verdict began to seem less and less likely . . .

Calvi had joined the Banco Ambrosiano at the age of twenty-six. He was an excellent linguist, and assisted in the closing of international deals. Some of Calvi's schemes netted the bank a great deal of money, and his promotion was fast: he rose from easing international transactions to becoming the bank's "central manager" in twenty years. Many people saw him as a cold and ruthless character – his wife maintained that he was merely shy. He was obsessed with the idea of *sottogoverno*, the secret interaction of hidden agencies and apparent political power. He carried a copy of Mario Puzo's *"The Godfather"* in his briefcase at all times, like a Bible.

Calvi was also ambitious, and despite his success he realized that he could not make the amount of money his ambition demanded managing a Catholic bank. He needed to deal in shares. The only problem was that Italian law did not allow banks to own shares, it being assumed that the temptation to siphon off other people's money into the bank's holdings would be too great. Calvi seemed to have reached a dead-end in his career.

In the late sixties Calvi met Michele Sindona, one of Italy's most successful financiers. Sindona had based a fortune upon Black Market trading during World War II. In the late fifties Mafia families in New York approached Sindona to launder some of their drug profits through investments in Italy. Sindona also had financial contacts in the Vatican. He had been made main financial adviser to the Vatican Bank, *uomo di fiducia*, when a friend, Cardinal Montini, became Pope in 1963.

Sindona was very useful to the Vatican Bank, as he could deal with matters that might appear too secular for the financial wing of a religious body. If any anti-religious groups, such as the communists, were to transact business with the Vatican, Sindona would be the negotiator, a secular frontman. He would attempt to disconnect inappropriate links and put the money into innocuous overseas holdings. A Vatican-owned company built the Watergate complex.

Sindona's closest link with the Vatican was Bishop Paul Marcinkus, secretary of the Vatican bank and bodyguard to the Pope. Marcinkus was a large American, born in Al Capone's Cicero. His association with Sindona profited both the Church and its adviser enormously.

When Sindona met Calvi in the late sixties he immediately recognized a man of ambition. He also correctly guessed that he would not mind becoming involved in transactions that were not one hundred per cent above board. Sindona, who owned many banks, had overcome the prohibition on his owning shares by setting up companies in "fiscal paradises" like Liechtenstein or Luxembourg and using these as a front for his own share deals. Now Calvi, in association with Sindona, began to avoid the Italian

Roberto Calvi, Italian banker and alleged member of the secret masonic lodge "P-2"

authorities' scrutiny in the same way. When Calvi opened a bank in South America the Italian banking overseers only found out about it through the newspapers.

Both Calvi and Sindona made a great deal of money through overseas share-holdings. The Bank of Italy seemed unwilling to interfere with their business. Only the oil crisis of 1973 brought an end to Sindona's world-spanning financial colonialism. He had planned to buy several extremely large banking institutions within Italy and merge them into the biggest single financial powerblock in the country. The worldwide crisis of confidence created by oil prices going up hit Sindona badly. The Franklin Bank, which Sindona owned, crashed in the biggest banking failure in American history. Sindona was charged with breaking American financial laws. The Vatican was rumoured to have lost $60 million in the crash. Marcinkus hastily declared that he hardly knew Sindona.

Calvi meanwhile was flourishing. He owned many banks and insurance companies. He had replaced Sindona as *uomo di fiducia* with the Vatican bank, and even bought a bank from them, the Banca Cattolico del Veneto. He planned to buy the bank that employed him, Banco Ambrosiano, through his foreign puppet companies. By 1975 he had became chairman and effectively owner of Banco Ambrosiano.

It was at this point that Calvi became involved with the Italian Freemason's lodge P2. The head of the lodge, Licio Gelli, offered Calvi membership, and on 23 August 1975 Calvi joined. P2 or Propaganda Two was an extremely powerful affiliation of members of government, businessmen and other people of influence. Gelli, a mysterious figure, was a kind of super-Mafia boss, in a position to grant favours to even the most powerful in the land. Calvi, with his prior interest in *sottogoverno* naturally saw membership of P2 as an essential accessory of power.

As Calvi was in the ascendant, Sindona's fortunes

foundered. Calvi was reluctant to financially re-establish his old partner — he had provided the $40 million with which Sindona had bought the Franklin bank — and did not want to throw good money after bad. Sindona anonymously informed the Bank of Italy of certain "questionable" deals struck between the Vatican Bank and Calvi. Spurred by these revelations, the Bank of Italy opened an investigation into Calvi's finances.

A greater problem was also about to assail Calvi. In August 1978 Pope Paul VI died. He was replaced by Albino Luciano, Pope John Paul I. Luciano had objected to Calvi's purchase of the Veneto Bank in 1974 and fully intended, now that he had the power, to investigate the Vatican Bank's dealings with Calvi and Sindona. However, Pope John Paul I died after only thirty-three days in the office. The medicines that he had been using during his sudden sickness were removed from his bedside table just after he died by Cardinal Villot, a member of P2. Calls for an autopsy were ignored and his body was hastily embalmed and interred. It has been argued that Luciano was poisoned. Whatever the case, the death must have been a great relief to Calvi.

The Bank of Italy's investigation soon foundered as well, as both the governor of the bank and the chief investigator into Calvi's accounts were arrested. Ironically, the charge was that they had not sufficiently investigated criminal actions of banks under their jurisdiction. Thus Calvi was saved any embarrassing results of the investigation becoming public.

At the same time a lawyer who was in charge of liquidating one of Sindona's Italian banks made some interesting discoveries regarding Calvi and the Vatican Bank. He found that the sale of the Veneto bank had involved a $6.5 million brokerage fee being paid to Marcinkus and Calvi. The day after he told writer Gianfranco Modolo his findings, he was shot dead in the street.

Sindona meanwhile had faced charges in the United States. He was found guilty on sixty-five counts of fraud and sentenced to twenty-five years in jail. Although Sindona was a member of P2, there was little that they could do for him in America. Also, P2 had problems of their own . . .

Mino Pecorelli, a member of P-2, had published articles hinting at a tax fraud perpetrated by Gelli and an oil magnate involving diesel. Gelli had found a way to sell domestic heating diesel, which is taxed at a low rate, as fuel for vehicles, which is heavily taxed. The money made had been laundered through Sindona and the Vatican Bank. Pecorelli did not realize the full extent of the scandal. When a fellow member of P2 tried to buy his silence, it became clear to Pecorelli that there was a great deal of money to be made blackmailing the Masons. He published an article revealing that Gelli had spied for the Communists during the war, and also that hinted at the extent of P2's influence. Within hours of the article hitting the news-stands, Pecorelli was dead, shot twice in the mouth while climbing into his car.

The hidden organization was beginning to become visible. In 1981, two magistrates investigating Sindona's connection with the Mafia came upon the name Licio Gelli. They ordered that his house be searched. In a safe was a list of P2's members. At first the investigator's thought that P2 was the plan for a *coup d'etat*. It soon dawned on them that P2 *was* a *coup d'etat*, it already controlled the actions of the state.

Gelli fled from Italy. The scandal brought down the Prime Minister Arnoldo Forlani. Calvi, whose name had been in the P2 file, was arrested.

Two share deals that Calvi had been involved in had led to the illegal export of billions of lire. Calvi struggled to keep Banco Ambrosiano from crashing, obtaining legitimate outside investment and himself investing in Italian business, but all avenues seemed closed. The Bank of Italy, for so long intimidated whenever it inquired into Calvi's funds, scented blood and demanded details of Calvi's foreign puppet companies. When the board of Banco Ambrosiano asked Calvi if they could see details of these companies themselves he flatly refused, and for the first time Calvi's board voted him down four to ten. On the morning of 11 June, Calvi disappeared.

Why he disappeared, and what he hoped to achieve are not known. It seems likely that he hoped to accumulate materials for his defence. What is known is that he drove halfway across Europe during the last week of his life. He

Eccentric billionaire James Gordon Bennett was so anxious to spend all his money that at one time he was actually found throwing thousand franc notes into the fire because they were bothering him when he sat down. In all, he managed to get through $10 million (about $280 million today). He once gave a guard on the Train Bleu between Paris and Monte Carlo a tip of $14,000 ($98,000 today).

The man immediately resigned and opened a restaurant. On another occasion he bought a restaurant in Monte Carlo on the spot because someone was sitting at his favourite table. The surprised owner agreed to sell to Bennett when he was offered $40,000 ($280,000 today). The millionaire then ordered the couple to leave his table at once, and after enjoying his favourite dish (Southdown mutton chops), he gave the waiter what was probably the biggest tip he would ever receive – the restaurant.

had contacted an associate called Silvano Vittor and obtained a false passport in the name of Gian Roberto Calvini. A Swiss businessman, Hans Kunz, organized low-key accommodation for Calvi in London at a block of serviced flats called the Chelsea Cloisters. Vittor and Calvi flew to London and checked into the hostel. From there Calvi telephoned his wife and seemed hopeful, saying that something had turned up that would help his defence. However, Calvi was still extremely nervous, refusing to leave his room and insisting that Vittor knocked in a pre-arranged fashion before he tried to enter.

On Thursday, 17 June 1982, a business associate of Calvi's called Carboni arrived at the Chelsea Cloisters and asked to speak to him. Calvi refused, and sent Vittor in his place. When Vittor returned, Calvi had gone. A few hours later he was found hanging under Blackfriars bridge.

A BBC team investigating the death established that Carboni's brother booked into a hotel in Geneva the previous night. On the evening after Calvi's death a private plane flew from Geneva to Gatwick, where it stayed only ninety minutes. On its return journey it had a briefcase on board. Calvi never travelled without his briefcase, but it was not found in the hotel room or at the scene of his "suicide". It contained, according to the BBC, papers detailing Calvi's dealings with the Vatican and P2. It has never been found.

In June 1983, a second inquest on Calvi in London preferred to return an open verdict on his death. That decision paid Calvi's widow $3 million in insurance money.

If Calvi was murdered who, then, was responsible? The question is difficult to answer, as so many people would have been pleased to see him out of the way. Calvi's wife believes that the Vatican was behind his murder. Italian Prime Minister Bettino Craxi has gone on the record as saying that Calvi was murdered by criminals associated with P2. It is certain that if Calvi had been prosecuted, the trial would have uncovered many details of Italy's huge *sottogoverno*. That, rather than Calvi's murder, is the real scandal.

When one examines the extent of the covert influence that moved the events of this story, it becomes easy to understand Calvi's fixation with *"The Godfather"*.

Thérèse Humbert:
the Impecunious Millionaire

Thérèse Humbert probably wins the prize for "con woman of all time". For her tale of dissimulation and deceit is worthy of any grand stage: she became one of the richest, most powerful people in nineteenth-century France by sealing up a safe and declaring that it contained a fortune which she was soon to inherit. Hardly a foolproof plan, but it worked. Creditors virtually queued at her door to give her money.

It was not even an original idea. Her father, Monsieur Aurignac, was fond of telling a tale or two, himself. And he wasn't choosy about whom he told them to. In particular, he enjoyed regaling his listeners with the fact that his name was not really Aurignac, but d'Aurignac, and his home was not the small cottage he lived in now but a mighty chateau in the Auvergne. Unfortunately, he had quarrelled most terribly with his parents and they had cast him out. But after his death, his children would inherit the castle, title and fortune of d'Aurignac. Unbelieving listeners were shown, as proof, a brass-studded chest, in which — he stated — lay all the documents necessary for his children to claim their fortune. On inspection after his death, the chest proved to contained nothing more than a brick.

It is not completely clear whether Thérèse had believed her father and was so mortified by his deception that she took up telling wild tales in the hope of one day regaining her fortune, or whether she simply wished to carry on the family tradition. However, there were other, more forceful, reasons as to why Thérèse began to lie for a living.

On the death of her father in 1874, the family — Thérèse was the eldest of four children — was forced to move to Toulouse to support itself. Her mother opened a small linen shop while Thérèse, not particularly enchanting in looks, started work as a washerwoman. To a child raised on dreams of the highest expectations, this was a crushing blow. For she knew that if she continued as a washerwoman she would end her days unmarried and poor. Furthermore, there were her brothers, Emile and Romain, and her sister, Marie, to support. She had to do something for all their sakes. She could not capture a rich husband with her looks, but there are other ways and Thérèse knew it. Her strength was her intelligence: she was sharp and persuasive. All she had to do was find the right man.

Working as a laundry maid in the house of Gustave Humbert, a prosperous lawyer and at that time Mayor of Toulouse, she found her ideal man: Gustave's son, Frédéric. Not only was he weak and insecure, he desperately needed to talk to someone. He was a sensitive, creative person, who wished to spend his days in the gentler pursuits, but his strict father had insisted that he train to become a lawyer. He wanted Frédéric to follow in his footsteps. It was terrible for Frédéric. Thérèse would murmur in sympathy, stroke his furrowed brow and say that she would help. For, she said, a kind old lady, Mademoiselle de Mariotte, had bequeathed to her a chateau, a large estate and riches beyond imagination. As soon as she turned twenty-one it would be hers and she would give it all to her dear Frédéric.

Her father had used that line a thousand times during his life, and never got anywhere. But Thérèse had chosen her target wisely. Frédéric was enchanted. For the first time in his life there was someone who cared about his feelings, and she was even prepared to give away all her money to help him. He proposed marriage. And when his father objected, on the grounds that she was tricking him and would never have two centimes to rub together, the couple eloped, married in secret and moved to Paris.

Although Thérèse could have been forgiven for counting her blessings and living out her life in comfort and some luxury, she had no intention of being so cautious. Once in Paris, the couple's lifestyle grew and grew in extravagance. They dined in the best restaurants, took the best seats in the theatre, and acquired property at an astounding rate. It was a lifestyle far beyond their means and which very soon brought them into trouble with their creditors. Matters were turning very nasty — it had long since become apparent, even to Frédéric, that there was no Mademoiselle or chateau — when Gustave Humbert, now the Minister of Justice who could not afford any scandals, stepped in and paid their debts. Thérèse and Frédéric were saved. The sight of hard cash had calmed the nerves of the creditors and Thérèse noted that they seemed even more eager to lend the Humberts money than before. It was a situation which had to be exploited.

A few months later, a windfall occurred. Thérèse had, it transpired, been left millions of dollars by a rich American, named Crawford. The reason for this good fortune? Thérèse had, as a young woman, been travelling on the Ceinture Railway in Paris when she fell to chatting to Mr Crawford, who was in France on holiday. She had been remarking on the sights to see, when he started to complain that he was not feeling very well. Thérèse, had kind heartedly taken him to her house and nursed him back to health: the illness having been worse than it at first appeared. So grateful had Mr Crawford been that he had duly included her in his will, unbeknown to her. Or, to be accurate, he had included Thérèse's sister Marie in his will: a girl he had never laid eyes upon.

Suspicions might have been raised at this point, especially bearing in mind the fictitious Mademoiselle de Mariotte and her chateau.

Besides, Thérèse would not be getting any money immediately, for there were certain conditions which had to be fulfilled. First of all, the legacy was tripartite. Marie was to receive a third of the estate, as were two cousins of Mr Crawford. Secondly, no part of the legacy was to be touched until Marie's twenty-first birthday. And last, but certainly not least, the will would not be valid unless one of the nephews married Marie.

However, Thérèse knew her audience. She might not be in full possession of the money quite yet, she stated, but she had been left all the necessary deeds and securities. All was needed was some patience. Marie would soon be twenty-one and neither of the Crawford nephews could fail to want such a charming girl for a wife.

Thérèse knew that she had to ensure that her story was believed by all. It was time to play her trump card. She and Frédéric had recently moved to a splendid house in the Avenue de la Grande Armée. In a blaze of publicity, she installed a fireproof safe in the bedroom of the mansion, hired a provincial magistrate to act as a notary and placed the documents and securities in the safe. The magistrate testified that the procedure had been above board and then Thérèse sealed the safe with hot wax. It would not be opened until Marie's twenty-first birthday. The inheritance was secure.

It was a brilliant move. All doubt vanished about the truth of her claim and Thérèse was able to borrow as much as she liked on the strength of it. She and Frédéric went on a spending spree that made their previous extravagance look shabby. They bought three country mansions and a steam yacht, countless hats and clothes and thousands of other things besides. In total, they borrowed 50 million francs, on the strength of an empty safe. Monsieur Aurignac would have smiled.

Scandals

Indeed, there was nothing of any worth inside the safe: the deeds and securities which Thérèse had placed in it had been forged by her brothers using fake letterheads.

Thérèse's deception grew: she borrowed using a promise of riches, and soon had the riches which enabled her to borrow even more. The initial 50 million francs which the legacy brought her helped her borrow almost twice as much again. In addition, if any creditor expressed reservations about the repayment of her loan, the conditions of the will, which initially could have brought her downfall, were now made to work for her. Various legal technicalities arose to slow down the inheritance process and explain the delay; the Crawford cousins could quibble about who was to marry Marie, and Marie herself might declare that she had no wish to marry either of the Americans. Thérèse Humbert was in crook's paradise. But she was not content with borrowing only from rich greedy Parisian bankers: she was out to obtain money from wherever she could. So she established an insurance company, the Rente Viagère.

Aimed very much at peasants and small businessmen and other people who were unable to save large amounts of money for their final days, it succeeded not simply because it offered large returns from small investments, but because it was seen to honour its settlements quickly and without fuss. Unfortunately for the investors, Rente Viagère was a sham. All deposits and payments received were left unsecured and any settlement which had to be paid was taken directly from these incoming payments. During its existence it took more than 40 million francs, most of which went into Thérèse's private bank account.

Unbeknown to Thérèse, however, the tide had turned. There was one weakness in her story: the Crawfords. Why no one had checked to see whether this family existed in the first place is a mystery, but it was done eventually. Monsieur Delatte, a banker from Lyons, travelled to America, discovered the truth and wrote to a friend detailing his findings. At first the friend did nothing, but when Monsieur Delatte was murdered, he confronted Thérèse and threatened to reveal the truth. Thérèse, using the full force of her powers, managed to persuade him to remain quiet, but she could not stop other people from following their suspicions. In particular, she could not stop Jules Bizat, an official at the Bank of France, because he did not confront her directly.

Intrigued by the workings of Rente Viagère, he started to make some enquiries and found out that while the company claimed to invest in gilt-edged securities, closer investigation proved otherwise. He nearly stayed silent, as he stood to lose personally from any damaging revelations: nearly every banker in France had lent money to Madame Humbert. But instead he made a visit to no less a person than Waldeck-Rousseau, the Prime Minister. The countdown to disaster had started for Madame Humbert.

It is a sign of how peculiarly powerful she now was that Waldeck-Rousseau did not act overtly against Thérèse. He preferred to undermine her position by leaking news of her financial misconduct to *Le Matin*. Normally, this would not have bothered Thérèse, but fate was starting to conspire against her. Before she could issue a denial, her lawyer, Monsieur De Buit, seemingly as convinced as anyone of Thérèse's innocence, decided to act. The safe would be opened, he declared. The truth will out.

How Thérèse must have cursed her luck. Her powers of persuasion had been so great that they led to her downfall. And that downfall was now assured, since there was nothing she could do to stop the opening of the safe: the date had been fixed and all of France was on tenterhooks. Thérèse started planning her escape. On 8 May, two days before the safe was due to be opened, her house mysteriously burnt down and the Humberts fled. Perhaps she thought the fire would wipe out the evidence, but she had overlooked one tiny detail: the safe really was fireproof!

Scandals

It remained intact, and on 10 May its contents were withdrawn, revealing a handful of worthless papers.

Seven months later, the authorities apprehended Frédéric, Thérèse, her brothers and sister. They were all accused of complicity in the frauds, although it was Thérèse whose name was repeated the most often. During the early part of 1903, the pressures rose, and in March, Marie was excused trial on the grounds that she had lost her mind and would not be able to answer with any kind of coherence. By that time Thérèse had already handled one court case — an Armenian had accused her of libel — and her actions had won her much support from the public. She was a feisty woman, and it seemed that she would go down fighting. That did not prove to be the case, however. The second trial, which opened on 8 August 1903, revealed a broken figure, who offered no resistance to the prosecution case. Two weeks later she was sentenced to five years in prison for her crimes, a sentence which was decidedly lighter than could have been expected, but which still seemed to fill her with dread. Frédéric, Émile, Romain and Marie were also found guilty on varying charges.

Thus came to an end one of the most incredible swindles of all time. For twenty years, Thérèse had enjoyed a life that only royalty can expect. But her years after prison were passed in neither luxury nor excitement, and she died an old, forgotten woman.

Chapter Three

Literary Fraud

I t is amazing how brilliant writers often resort to untruths to get noticed. They sensationalize the contents of their books to get accepted, and then find themselves in a dilemma when they realize that a follow-up book is wanted, and they have to embellish even more to continue the story.

Mikhail Sholokhov – The Quiet Flows the Don Plagiarism Scandal

The most eminent Russian author to emerge since the Revolution in 1917 is undoubtedly Mikhail Alexandrovitch Sholokhov, born in the hamlet of Kruzhlino, on the banks of the Don, in 1905. Like Gorky, Sholokhov led a varied life – soldier, handyman, statistician, food inspector, goods handler, mason, book-keeper and finally journalist – before he hurtled to literary fame at the age of twenty-three with the first volume of *Tikhi Don*, *The Quiet Don* (translated into English as *Quiet Flows the Don*). When compared with the great Russian novels of the nineteenth century, it seems full of "shock tactics" of the kind associated with cheap popular novels in England and the United States. The book begins with a scene in which the Turkish wife of a Cossack is trampled by a mob who believe her to be a witch. As a result she dies in premature childbirth. Shortly thereafter there is a description of how a seventeen-year-old girl is raped by her father and how her brother and mother then beat and kick him to death. Seductions, rapes and various forms of violence follow at regular intervals. But the nature of the writing is as fine as anything in the work of the novelist Turgenev.

Sholokhov's first book *Tales of the Don* appeared when he was only twenty. It is interesting to note in these tales of the civil war and shortly after that, the village leaders are portrayed as isolated from the people; later, as he learned communist conformity, Sholokhov showed them integrated with the people.

Sholokhov began work on *Tikhi Don* when he was twenty-one. When it appeared two years later – and became an instant bestseller – critics were amazed that anyone so young could write so powerfully; it eventually sold four and a half million copies before its fourth and final volume appeared fourteen years later. The later volumes are generally admitted to be inferior to the first. *Virgin Soil Upturned* (1932), about a collective farm, was a success in Russia but it is considered inferior to the earlier parts of *Tikhi Don*.

Soon after the first volume of *Tikhi Don* appeared in 1925, rumours began to spread around Moscow literary circles to the effect that Sholokhov was not the true author and that he had found the manuscript or a diary on which he based the book. In 1929, *Pravda* published a letter from a number of proletarian writers denouncing the "malicious slander". It even threatened prosecution. Nevertheless, Sholokhov was generally regarded as Russia's most important writer. In 1965 he was given the Nobel Prize for literature. By then, Sholokhov had become spokesman for the Soviet literary establishment, denouncing writers like Pasternak and Solzhenitsyn and taking an aggressively anti-intellectual stand that has caused young writers to regard him with distaste. This may be fuelled by envy for his life style on a large estate at Rostov-on-Don, where he has a private aeroplane and theatre, and hunts regularly.

Alexander Solzhenitsyn, who was forced into exile in Zurich in 1974, brought out of Russia a number of documents about Sholokhov's work by a friend whom he identifies simply as "D". "D", according to Solzhenitsyn, engaged in painstaking literary analysis of *Tikhi Don* but died before he could complete it. Solzhenitsyn explained that he could not reveal "D's" real name for fear of reprisals against his family but he published the manuscript and appealed to Western scholars to help complete the research.

"D's" textual analysis revealed two different authors of *Tikhi Don*: some 95 per cent of its first two volumes belong to the "original author", while less than 70 per cent of the second two are his work. "D's" scepticism was apparently aroused by the fact that the first two volumes, which showed intimate acquaintance with pre-Revolutionary society in the Don region and described World War I and the Civil War, were allegedly written by a young man between the ages of twenty-one and twenty-three. Sholokhov was too young to have witnessed either war. Even the

In December 1926, the novelist Agatha Christie disappeared from her home in Sunningdale, Berkshire. Twelve days later her husband tracked her down to an hotel in Harrogate – a waiter had recognized her. The press was told that she had suffered a loss of memory – it was true that her husband was having an affair with another woman at the time, and she was under considerable emotional pressure. But from then on, her detective novels – so far hardly noticed – began to enjoy increasing sales. Was her disappearance a deliberate publicity stunt, as many have alleged? For the rest of her life, Agatha Christie flatly refused to discuss the matter.

speed of composition seems incredible – a novel of well over a quarter of a million words had been written in two years. Yet it took another fourteen years to complete the remaining two volumes and the first part of *Virgin Soil Upturned*. Sholokhov seemed to have "dried up". His collected works, issued in honour of his seventy-fifth birthday in 1980, amounted to a mere eight volumes.

According to Solzhenitsyn, (introducing "D's" book *The Mainstream of the Quiet Don*) the true author of *Tikhi Don* was a historian of the Don region, one Fyodor Dmitrievitch Kryukov, born in 1870, the son of a local "ataman" (village leader). By the end of the nineteenth century he had achieved great popularity as a recorder of Cossack life and was elected to the state parliament (Duma). Solzhenitsyn believes he began writing his major work, *Tikhi Don*, in Petrograd during World War I. As a Cossack, he was opposed to the Bolsheviks who seized power in 1917 and fought with the army of the Don. When this collapsed, he retired to the Kuban and died there of typhoid at the age of fifty. "D's" analysis of Kryukov's earlier works, which were never reprinted by the Soviet regime, convinced him that he was the true author of *Tikhi Don* and that as a journalist Sholokhov somehow came across Kryukov's manuscript and used it as a basis for his own book, deleting whole chapters where they did not suit his purpose and inserting material of his own. This, according to "D", explains the unevenness of the style and various internal contradictions.

Understandably, the Soviet view is that Solzhenitsyn is merely concerned with slandering and undermining the greatest Soviet novelist. But if this is so, at least he has presented his evidence in full so it can be studied by literary scholars and experts who can decide on its merits.

Lobsang Rampa – The "Third Eye" Hoax

Some time in 1955, a man arrived at the office of the publisher Secker and Warburg in Great Russell Street, London, and managed to persuade its chairman, Fred Warburg, to see him. The man, who wore a tonsure, introduced himself as Dr T. Lobsang Rampa, and explained that he had written his autobiography and wanted Mr Warburg to publish it. He declared he was a medical doctor and produced a document, in English, which he said was issued by the University of Chungking. Mr Warburg agreed to look at the manuscript, which thereafter arrived in sections. It was a fascinating document describing how the young Rampa, child of wealthy parents, had been singled out by astrologers at the age of seven to become a monk and how he had trained in a monastery. At the age of eight, he had submitted to a brain operation to open the "third eye" – the source of man's psychic powers. A hole was drilled in his forehead, then a sliver of very hard wood poked into this brain, so he saw "spirals of colour and globules of incandescent smoke". "For the rest of your life you will see people as they are and not as they pretend to be." And Rampa saw, to his astonishment, that all the men in the room were surrounded by a luminous golden flame, the vital aura.

Warburg had his doubts; the details seemed authentic, but the style was curiously English and colloquial. "I really did not think so much of kite-flying. Stupid idea, I thought. Dangerous. What a way to end a promising career. This is where I go back to prayers and herbs . . ." It didn't sound Tibetan. Various experts expressed contradictory opinions. But Rampa stood by his story of being a Tibetan. Warburg submitted him to a test: a few words of Tibetan. Rampa agreed that he could not understand it but explained that there was a perfectly good reason. During World War II he had been a prisoner of the Japanese, who had tortured him for information about his country; he had used his psychic powers to blot out all his knowledge of Tibetan.

Warburg swallowed his doubts and published, and the results vindicated his commercial sense. The book became a bestseller. It went into many languages and made Rampa a rich man.

A body of "Tibetan scholars" was doubtful about its authenticity and hired a private detective, Clifford Burgess, to find out about Lobsang Rampa. What he discovered was that Rampa was in reality Cyril Henry Hoskins, a Devon man who now lived in Thames Ditton. Hoskins had been born in Plympton, near Plymouth, in 1911, and entered his father's plumbing business. He was apparently deeply interested in psychic matters and claimed to have been taken to China as a child. It seemed that Hoskins was given to fantasizing about China and things Chinese; a journalist on *Psychic News*, John Pitt, tracked down a couple who had known him when he was a clerk in Weybridge and was told that Hoskins had claimed to be a flying instructor in the Chinese air force and had had an accident when his parachute failed to open. Later still, Hoskins changed his name to Carl Kuon Suo, called himself Dr Kuon, and claimed to have been born in Tibet.

Fred Warburg was understandably dismayed by these revelations but pointed out that he had published a note in the book saying that the author took full responsibility for all statements made in it. And he hinted at an alternative theory. "But is the truth, the whole truth, out? . . . Did he believe his own fantasies? Was he, perhaps, the mouthpiece of a true Lama, as some have alleged?" Rampa/Hoskins was tracked down to a house outside Dublin, where he was living with a lady whom he had, apparently, seduced away from her Old Etonian husband. Rampa declined to be interviewed; so did the Old Etonian husband.

In 1917, two girls, Frances Wright and Elsie
Griffiths, cut some pictures of fairies out of a
magazine, borrowed a camera and photographed
Elsie surrounded by the fairies. It was just a
little bit of fun and they soon forgot about the
photographs. But one way or another, news
leaked out that real fairies had been captured on
camera. All of a sudden the Cottingley Fairies
were famous.

Both Frances and Elsie must have believed
that the truth would soon be discovered, but it
amused them to remain quiet and see what
happened. And how they must have chuckled as
expert after expert queued up to verify the
little creatures. Indeed, such was the fervour
with which they were acclaimed that many
people still believed that they were real, until
the two women finally broke their silence in
1976.

Quite undeterred by the furore, Rampa went on to write
a second book, *Doctor From Lhasa* (1959), which was
accepted by Souvenir Press. The publisher's note in this
book acknowledged that *The Third Eye* had caused great
contention but went on to state that the author's explanation was that he had been "possessed" by the Tibetan lama
Rampa, since a blow on the head had caused mild concus-
sion, and that Rampa now wrote his books through the
author. Whatever the truth of the matter, the publisher
added diplomatically, it is right that the book should be
available to the public . . . *Doctor From Lhasa* continued the
story where *The Third Eye* left off but is even more
incredible. There is, for example, a chapter describing
how Rampa jumped into an aircraft and, without any

flying lessons, flew around for an hour or so, then brought the plane in to land.

Doctor From Lhasa revealed that Rampa had an audience who would believe anything he said. In a third book, *The Rampa Story*, he continued Rampa's autobiography from the point where he had left off at the end of the previous book — where Rampa was a prisoner of the Japanese and narrowly escaped execution — and described how he crossed into Russian territory, was imprisoned in the Lubianka prison in Moscow, then escaped, via Europe, to America. But the high point of the book is its seventh chapter, where Rampa described leaving his body and soaring to the astral plane, where his old teacher, the Lama Mingyar Dondup, was awaiting him. Dondup tells him: "Your present body has suffered too much and will shortly fail. We have established a contact in the Land of England. This person wants to leave his body. We took him to the astral plane and discussed matters with him. He is *most* anxious to leave, and will do all we require . . ." Later, in London, Rampa is able to study the history of this Englishman in the Akashic record — the record on the "psychic ether" of everything that has ever happened (Madame Blavatsky invented the phrase). Then Rampa goes to the Englishman's bedroom — in his astral body — and converses with the Englishman's astral body, agreeing to the swap. The Englishman tells him how he fell on his head and stood up to find himself standing by his physical body, connected to it by a silver cord. Then he saw a Tibetan walking towards him. "I have come to you because I want your body . . ." And, after thinking it over, the unselfish Mr Hoskins decided that he had had enough of life anyway, and that he might as well hand over his body to someone who could make better use of it. The lama instructs him to climb the tree again and fall on his head in order to loosen the cord. Then a lama takes Hoskins by the arm and floats away with him to heaven, while Lobsang Rampa squeezes himself into the vacated body with a sensation of suffocating. Rampa finds himself confronted with such problems as riding a bicycle and claiming unemployment benefit. Life was difficult and painful until he met a literary agent and outlined the story of *The Third Eye* . . .

The book should end there, but there is more to tell. After finishing *The Third Eye* he has a heart attack, and he and his wife move to Ireland. (It is not clear why the climate of Ireland should be better for heart ailments than England.) There he wrote *Doctor From Lhasa*. But the task was still not completed; he had to go on and tell *The Rampa Story*. Driven out of Ireland by income tax problems, he moves to Canada. There he receives a telepathic message: he must go on writing and tell the *Truth*. "Write it down, Lobsang, and also write of what *could* be in Tibet." And he continues to tell a story of how Truth found it difficult to obtain an audience until he borrowed the coloured garments of Parable. After that, Truth was welcome everywhere . . . (This, presumably, is intended as a reply to people who claim that Rampa's Tibet is unlike the real place; he can always claim he is talking in parables.) The book ends with a nasty vision of an atomic rocket, launched from Tibet by the Chinese. "Is it fantasy?" he asks. "It could be fact." The placing of the quotation suggests that it could refer to the whole Rampa story.

Rampa's explanations about his body swap must have convinced a fair number of readers, for he has gone on to produce several more books: *Cave of the Ancients, Living With a Lama, You-Forever, Wisdom of the Ancients*, and a book called *My Visit to Venus* in which he describes how he was taken to Venus in a flying saucer and spent some time studying the history of Atlantis and Lemuria in its sky-scraper cities. (Space probes have since shown that Venus is too hot to support any form of life.)

It seems that Hoskins has constructed a story that cannot be disproved by the sceptics, since he has an answer to every objection. Yet there still remain a few matters that need explaining. Why did Hoskins tell his neighbours, a Mr and Mrs Boxall, in 1943 or 1944, that he had been a pilot in the Chinese air force?

This was some years before his first "meeting" with Lobsang Rampa. And why, in 1948, did he change his name to Dr Carl Kuon Suo, rather than to Lobsang Rampa? Of one thing we can be sure: Rampa would have no difficulty providing answers that would satisfy the faithful.

Carlos Castaneda – The Don Juan Hoax

In 1968, the University of California Press published a book called *The Teachings of Don Juan: A Yacqui Way of Knowledge*, by Carlos Castaneda. Castaneda had entered the University of California – UCLA – as an undergraduate in 1959, and had received a BA in anthropology in 1962. The University of California Press accepted *The Teachings of Don Juan* as an authentic account of Castaneda's 'field work' in Mexico. The book told how, when he was an anthropology student, in 1960, Castaneda made several trips to the southwest to collect information on medicinal plants used by the Indians. At a Greyhound bus station, he was introduced to a white-haired old Indian who apparently knew all about peyote, the hallucinogenic plant. Although this first meeting was abortive – Castaneda tells with touching honesty how he "talked nonsense" to Don Juan – Castaneda made a point of finding out where Don Juan lived and was finally accepted by the old *brujo* (medicine man or magician) as a pupil, a sorcerer's apprentice. The teaching begins with an episode in which Don Juan tells Castaneda to look for his "spot", a place where he will feel more comfortable and at ease than anywhere else; he told Castaneda that there was such a spot within the confines of the porch. Castaneda describes how he spent all night trying different spots, lying in them, but felt no difference. Don Juan told him he ought to use his eyes. After this, he began to distinguish various colours in the darkness: purple, green and verdigris. When he finally chose one of these, he felt sick and had a sensation of panic. Exhausted, he lay by the wall and fell asleep. When he woke up, Don Juan told him that he had found his "spot" – where he had fallen asleep. The other spot was bad for him, the "enemy".

This episode helps to explain the subsequent popularity of the book which was published in paperback by Ballantine Books and sold 300,000 copies. Don Juan is a teacher, a man of knowledge – the kind of person that every undergraduate dreams of finding – and he introduces Castaneda to the most astonishing experiences. When Castaneda first eats a peyote button, he experiences amazing sensations and plays with a mescalito god whose mind he can read. On a later occasion he sees the mescalito god himself as a green man with a pointed head. When Don Juan teaches him how to make a paste from the *datura* plant – Jimson weed – he anoints himself with it and has a sensation of flying through the air at a great speed. (In their book *The Search for Abraxas*, Stephen Skinner and Neville Drury speculate that witches of the Middle Ages used a similar concoction and that this explains how they "flew" to Witches' Sabbaths.) He wakes up to find himself half a mile from Don Juan's house.

During the period when the book was published every young American was smoking pot and experimenting with "psychedelic drugs" like mescalin and LSD, and Timothy Leary was advising American youth to "Turn on, tune in, drop out." This apparently factual account of semi-magical experiences became as popular as Tolkien's *Lord of the Rings* and for much the same reason: it was escapist literature, but, more important, it claimed to be true.

Reviews were excellent. Anthropologists and scientists took the book seriously – the psychologist Carl Rogers called it "one of the most vividly convincing documents I have read". The philosopher Joseph Margolis said that either Castaneda was recording an encounter with a master or he was himself a master.

This was clearly a success that had to be followed up. *A Separate Reality* described how Castaneda had returned to Don Juan in 1968. A giant gnat, 100 feet high, circles round him; he rides on a bubble; he has a semi-mystical experience in which he hears extraordinary sounds and sees the sorcerer's "ally", who shows him a "spirit catcher".

The demand for more about Don Juan remained strong but Castaneda had a problem. *A Separate Reality* came to an end in 1970 and was published in 1971; for the time being he had used up his Don Juan material. But not quite. He explained in his next book, *Journey to Ixtlan* (1973) that he had made the erroneous assumption that the glimpses of reality that Don Juan had given him could only be obtained through drugs. Now he realized he was mistaken. In fact, Don Juan had told him many other things during his years as a sorcerer's apprentice, but although he had written these non-drug revelations in his "field notes", he had failed to see their significance. Now, looking back over his notes, he realized that he had a vast amount of material that showed that drugs were not necessary for achieving unusual states of consciousness. So *Journey to Ixtlan* goes back to 1960 and recounts still more astonishing adventures: he has strange visions, mountains move, and Castaneda describes his encounter with a sinister but beautiful sorceress named Catalina.

In retrospect, it seems that Castaneda made his first major error in writing *Ixtlan* (although it was one that, according to his agent, made him $1 million). The "lost" field notes sound just a little too convenient. Yet, oddly enough, scholars continued to take him seriously. Mary Douglas, a professor of social anthropology, wrote an article about the first three books called "The Authenticity of Castaneda", which concluded: "From these ideas we are likely to get advances in anthropology." Moreover, UCLA granted Castaneda his Ph.D for *Ixtlan* and he lectured on anthropology on the Irvine campus.

If reviewers would swallow Ixtlan they would clearly swallow anything. Now that enough time had elapsed since his last visit to Sonora, Castaneda could renew his acquaintance with Don Juan and bring his revelations up to date. But *Tales of Power* (1974) seems to indicate that either Castaneda or his publisher felt that the game would soon be up. The dust jacket declares that this is the "culmination of Castaneda's extraordinary initiation into the mysteries of sorcery". At last, it declares, Castaneda completes his long journey into the world of magic and the book ends with a "deeply moving farewell". In many ways *Tales of Power* — covering a period of a few days in 1971 — is more rewarding than the earlier Don Juan books because it attempts to present a philosophical theory about reality, in terms of two concepts which Don Juan calls the *tonal* and the *nagual*. The *tonal* is "everything we are", while the *nagual* is pure potentiality. The *tonal* is the pair of Kantian spectacles through which we see the world and impose meaning on it; it consists mainly of linguistic concepts and preconceptions. These conceptions are illustrated with the usual tales of magical experiences: Don Juan shows him a squirrel wearing spectacles which swells until it is enormous and then disappears; Carlos walks a few steps and finds he has travelled one and a half miles.

It was at this point, after publication of *Tales of Power*, that a teacher of psychology named Richard de Mille was persuaded by his niece to read all four Don Juan books one after the other. ("You have to take the whole trip.") *The Teachings* struck him as authentic and factual. *A Separate Reality* raised doubts; it was better written but somehow not so "factual". And the character of Don Juan had changed; he seemed more "joky", while in the first book he had been grimly serious. Of course, Castaneda himself had already mentioned this. "He clowned during the truly crucial moments of the second cycle." But when he came to *Ixtlan*, De Mille was puzzled to find that the Don Juan of the notes made as early as 1960 was as much of a humorist and a clown as the later Don Juan. Made suspicious by this inconsistency, he began to study the books more closely and soon found contradictions that confirmed his feeling that he was dealing with fiction rather than fact. A friend pointed out one obvious inconsistency: in October 1968 Castaneda leaves his car and walks for two days to the shack of Don Juan's fellow sorcerer Don Genaro but when they walk out of the shack they climb straight into the car. De Mille discovered a similar contradiction. In *Ixtlan*, Castaneda goes looking for a certain bush on Don Juan's instructions and finds it has vanished; then Don Juan leads him to the far side of the hill, where he finds the bush he thought he had seen earlier on the other side. Later Don Juan tells him, "This morning you *saw*", giving the word special emphasis. Yet six years later, in 1968, Castaneda is represented (in *A Separate Reality*) as asking Don Juan what is *seeing* and Don Juan tells him that in order to find out, Castaneda must *see* for himself. He seems to have forgotten that Castaneda had an experience of *seeing* six years earlier. And while it is understandable that Don Juan should forget, it is quite incomprehensible that Castaneda should.

These and many similar inconsistencies convinced De Mille that one of the two books had to be fiction, or that, more probably, they both were. He published his results in a book called *Castaneda's Journey* in 1976 and it led many anthropologists who had taken Don Juan seriously to change their views. Joseph K. Long felt "betrayed by Castaneda". Marcello Truzzi, on the other hand, admitted that he had felt aghast at the initial reactions of the scientific community to Castaneda's books and that he was equally outraged by the lack of serious reaction now De Mille had exposed them as frauds.

Castaneda's admirers were mostly infuriated. Their feeling was that even if Castaneda had invented Don Juan, the books were full of genuine knowledge and wisdom, and should be gratefully accepted as works of genius. One lady wrote to De Mille saying she was convinced he didn't exist and asking him to prove it. De Mille had, in fact, accepted that the Don Juan books had a certain merit, both as literature and as "occult teaching". But when, in 1980, he edited a large volume of essays on the "Castaneda hoax" called *The Don Juan Papers* his admiration had visibly dwindled. Some of the essays present an even more devastating exposure of Castaneda than De Mille's original volume: for example, Hans Sebald, an anthropologist who had spent a great deal of time in the southwestern desert, pointed out that it was so hot from June to September that no one with any sense ventures into it; dehydration and exhaustion follow within hours. Yet according to Castaneda, he and Don Juan wandered around the desert for days, engaged in conversation and ignoring the heat. Sebald goes on to demolish Castaneda's animal lore: "Where . . . are the nine-inch centipedes, the tarantulas big as saucers? Where are the king snakes, scarlet racers, chuckawallas, horned toads, gila monsters . . .?" A lengthy appendix to *The Don Juan Papers* cites hundreds of parallel passages from the Castaneda books and from other works on anthropology and mysticism that bear a close resemblance. The book establishes, beyond all possible doubt, that the Castaneda books are a fraud.

Richard De Mille's own researches revealed that Carlos Arana was born in 1925 (not 1935, as he has told an interviewer) in Cajamarca, Peru, and came to San Francisco in 1951, leaving behind a Chinese-Peruvian wife who was pregnant. In 1955 he met Damon Runyon's distant cousin Margaret and married her; they separated after six months. In 1959 he became an undergraduate at UCLA and the Don Juan story begins . . .

Scandals

Castaneda himself has proved to be an extremely elusive individual, as *Time* discovered when it sent a reporter to interview him in 1973. In the light of De Mille's discoveries this is easy to understand. Castaneda's career can be compared to that of the Shakespeare forger, William Ireland, who began by forging a few Shakespeare signatures to gain his father's attention and found himself forced to continue until he had concocted a whole new Shakespeare play, which brought about his discovery and downfall. Castaneda presumably produced the original *Teachings of Don Juan* as a mild form of hoax. The publication by Ballantine launched him, whether he liked it or not, on the career of a trickster and confidence man. It would, perhaps, have been wiser to stop after *Ixtlan*, or possibly *Tales of Power*. But the demand for more Don Juan books has presumably overcome his caution. In fact, the fifth, *The Second Ring of Power*, reads so obviously as fiction that it raises the suspicion that Castaneda wanted to explode his own legend. But he shows caution in offering no dates, no doubt to escape De Mille's vigilant eye. Castaneda tells how he went back to Mexico looking for Don Juan and instead encountered one of his disciples, a sorceress named Madame Solitude. Last time he saw her she was fat and ugly and in her fifties; now she is young, slim and vital, and within a few pages, she has torn off her skirt and invited him to make love to her — an invitation he wisely resists. Then Castaneda somehow invokes his own double out of his head — not a mild-mannered scholar but a super-male authority figure who hits Madame Solitude on the head and almost kills her. Then four lady disciples arrive and make more assaults on Castaneda, which he overcomes, and after which they all encounter other-worldly beings . . .

In his sixth book, *The Eagle's Nest*, Castaneda returns to Mexico as "a sorcerous leader and figure in his own right" (as the blurb says) and enters into a closer relationship with one of the female sorcerers of the previous book, La Gorda.

The two of them develop the ability to dream in unison. It is clear that, since writing the earlier book, Castaneda has come across split-brain physiology and now we hear a great deal about the right and left sides of a human being, the left being the *nagual* and the right the *tonal*. De Mille had pointed out that the Don Juan books seem to chart Castaneda's literary and philosophical discoveries over the years and this book confirms it. For those who read it with the certainty that the previous books were a hoax, it seems an insult to the intelligence. But it seems to demonstrate that Castaneda can continue indefinitely spinning fantasies for those who regard him as the greatest of modern gurus.

William Henry Ireland – the Second Shakespeare

A famous English playwright told a tale of the murder of a goodly king by a depraved tyrant, of the love of that tyrant's daughter for the rightful heir, and of the treacherous battles which ensued before order was restored. Who could it be, but Shakespeare? That is, of course, what William Henry Ireland wanted people to think when he put pen to paper in the late eighteenth century. Or, more accurately, that is what he wanted his father to think. For this fraud was not set in motion for any monetary gain. There was no bitterness towards the literary critics, or society in general. The only point William wished to prove was that he was a worthy son and heir to his father Samuel, who, in his capacity as an antiquarian bookseller, cared deeply about Shakespeare and not a jot about his son.

The reason we know about this fake and others perpetrated by Ireland is mostly to do with the intense reverence with which the eighteenth century regarded the Bard and the zeal with which it greeted any Shakespearean memento, however small. His will had been joyously discovered in 1747; a mulberry tree planted by the bard himself was dissected and distributed to an excited crowd ten years later. And there were numerous Shakespearean festivals each year, the most conspicuous of which were held in Stratford and in Drury Lane, London. Naturally, the uncovering of a complete new play was bound to have far reaching repercussions.

The climate for fraud, then, was perfect; but was Ireland up to the task? After all, his father, when he was not disowning him, reckoned him a dullard with no talent whatsoever, a waste of time. Throughout William's childhood, his father not only refused to believe the boy was his, but used the possible disclosure of his true father as a threat to keep the boy in his place. Regardless of whether or not his view of William's abilities was correct, it is hard to believe that a true literary talent could flourish in such an oppressive atmosphere. Yet, fortunately for William, he was educated for the most part in post-revolutionary France, a society in which there was much intellectual debate and where his desire to be a writer was hatched.

It was in 1793, while on a buying trip with his father – who had begrudgingly let him come along – that William saw his chance to pursue both his ambitions: to gain the respect of his father and to become a writer. One night, Ireland senior pontificated at length on Shakespeare's virtues, letting slip what a great achievement it would be to unearth even a fragment of the Bard's handiwork. The point was not lost on William. It was he who should make the discovery.

A year later, William produced a title deed to a property near the Old Globe Theatre. Its importance lay in the fact that the contract was between an actor, John Heminge, and William Shakespeare. As fakes go, it was pretty poor: William simply wrote Heminge's signature with his left hand! Nevertheless, it was pronounced genuine by various experts and it paved the way for a series of Shakespeare finds over the next couple of months. They came from the same source, a conveniently publicity shy Mr H. who had asked William to sort through his papers. Again, hardly a well thought out excuse. Had anyone checked, William's fraud would have been over almost before it began. But, as with many frauds, fortune favoured the brave. Samuel Ireland, overjoyed by this good fortune, championed the finds and they were soon the talk of the town.

The new memorabilia covered a variety of topics and were much more substantial than the initial discovery. Some illuminated the personal side of the playwright, revealing his correspondence with the Earl of Southampton, his love poetry written for Anne Hathaway, and even a letter from Elizabeth the First. The main bulk, however, was from his professional life. Uncovered were two theatre contracts, the original manuscripts of *Hamlet* and *King Lear*, and his "Profession of Faith" (which moved Boswell to tears). And to cap these all, there was a previously unknown play, the *Vortigern*.

Interest in every household in the country had been aroused. When Samuel Ireland put them on show, thousands flocked to gaze upon the treasures. Many experts, including Boswell and the poet laureate, Henry Pye, stated that the articles were genuine and even the Royal Family warmed to them. In an atmosphere of euphoria such as this, the fact that many great literary critics, particularly Edmond Malone, did not give them credit as genuine seems not to have mattered. William had inadvertently given the public what they wanted and they were going to believe in it, come what may.

Two men, Kemble, the actor/manager of the Drury Lane Theatre, and Sheridan, the theatre's owner, understood this well and snapped *Vortigern* up for production sometime during 1795. They believed it to be a fake, and not a particularly good one at that, but it would be good box office stuff. The theatre, they reasoned, would be full whatever verdict was finally delivered. And if they had staged the play in that year, there is every reason to believe that it would have had a long and successful run. However, as was to happen with Clifford Irving two centuries later, Ireland's luck began to turn. In December 1795, an authentic signature of John Heminge was brought to light. Unsurprisingly, it was completely different to Ireland's left handed attempt. Not in itself damning evidence, because the signature could just as easily have been fraudulent as real. But it sowed the seeds of doubt, which were given further sustenance by Edmond Malone's impending work *Inquiry into the validity of the Papers attributed to Shakespeare*. In it, he was known to have compiled a whole section devoted to *Vortigern* and its inconsistencies.

By January 1796, Ireland's former supporters were changing their allegiance. Both the *Oracle* and the *Monthly Mirror* condemned the finds and, more importantly, the crowds that had thronged outside the showroom were dwindling. Production of *Vortigern* had been delayed until March or April of that year and there was much debate as to why Ireland had, so far, only shown the transcript in modern copy form. Kemble and Sheridan, sensing the change in tides, began to ask for their money back and said that they would only proceed if the original manuscript was produced. It appeared that Ireland's fraud had stumbled and fallen. He could not produce the original manuscript, he could not prove Heminge's signature a fake, nor could he answer the one query which Malone, in advance of his book, had raised.

This last point seemed to be the final nail in the coffin. Malone had analyzed the letters carefully, especially that which purported to be from Elizabeth the First. Why, he asked, does the Queen state that she is expecting the Earl of Leicester at the Globe Theatre, when, at the time of the letter's writing, the Earl of Leicester had been dead for six years?

Yet, just when all appeared lost, there came succour from the Royal Family. The Duke of Clarence (whose mistress was Dorothea Jordan, the female lead in the *Vortigern*) exclaimed that the findings were most definitely sprung from Shakespeare's hand and that the Drury Lane Theatre had better proceed as quickly as possible with the staging of the new play. The old manuscript would be produced in due course, but for the moment the modern transcript should be used. At the time, this must have seemed like divine intervention, although, given the eventual fate of the play, it might have been better for Ireland if the Duke had stayed aloof.

The date fixed for the opening night, 2 April, would be, it was hoped, some weeks before the publication of Malone's book, thus giving the play time to gain the support it would need to survive. In practice, this did not happen as Malone's book came out on 31 March. The spotlight was thrown onto the play, and although Samuel Ireland (who would remain convinced of the findings' authenticity, even after William had confessed) was unconcerned and simply added a footnote urging the public to be judge, this time it was really the beginning of the end. Despite a last minute show of support for *Vortigern* from some twenty literary dignitaries, the play was torn apart by the actors and audience alike. It survived as a serious work for the first act, but after that, with Kemble leading the way, the actors hammed their lines up and egged the audience on to greater and greater shows of ridicule. It was the first and last night of *Vortigern*'s stage performance. The public had given their judgement, reserving their worst humiliation for the Duke of Clarence by pelting him with oranges, as he rather drunkenly tried to defend the play.

In the days that followed, Malone's book provided more and more examples of inconsistencies and errors, such as spelling mistakes, anachronisms, impossible dates and meetings. The fraud was well and truly exposed. The fraudster, however, was not.

Scandals

If William Ireland had had the same motives as Irving or Keating or van Meegeren, then he could have considered himself a success. But his forgeries had not been executed for any other reason than to gain the respect of a man, who still, after twenty-one years, did not recognize him as his son and did not credit him with any talent. It was frustrating and hurtful, and, not surprisingly, William could not keep his secret hidden any longer. He wanted to show his father just how ingenious he had been and he wanted to receive some recognition for that ingenuity. Consequently, in May 1796, he announced to Samuel Ireland that he alone could vouch for the findings, that he alone knew the identity of Mr H. To his bitter regret, he got no reaction from his father. Finally, unable to bear this silence anymore, William revealed that he himself was the author. Sadly, even this failed to win his father over, as the very papers William had forged had become Samuel's life. All that the son obtained was a brief argument rejecting both Malone's criticisms and William himself. They never talked to one another again.

Unlike Irving, Keating and van Meegeren, Ireland was not sentenced to prison. However, his demise is somehow more distressing. All three of the other fraudsters became folk-heroes in their own right. They were all recognized as masters of their art, albeit an unusual one. Ireland saw none of this but it was he who really desired it. In addition, his prolific writing skills — he had already written "Shakespeare"'s *Henry II* and had been in the process of starting his *William the Conqueror* when the *Vortigern* dived so disastrously that April night — were never given an outlet. He was, truly, a tragic figure.

Chapter Four

How Have
the Mighty Fallen

*T*hey may be famous but it doesn't mean they can get away *with anything — even if they may think so. A rail ticket scandal, where a "professor" was found not to have a ticket for his journey and then tried to buy one from the ticket collector for only part of his journey; or the famous actor who tried to swindle more petrol rations from the government for his Rolls-Royce during the war. Because they were in the public eye, they thought they were above the law.*

Heinrich Schliemann –
The Great Troy Hoax

During his lifetime and for more than eighty years after his death, in 1890, the name of Heinrich Schliemann – "the man who found Troy" – remained untainted by the slightest breath of scandal. The discovery in the late 1970s that he was, in fact, a pathological liar and a crook caused tremendous reverberations in the world of archaeology.

Heinrich Schliemann, the man who was to be described as "the creator of prehistoric Greek archaeology", was born on 6 January 1822 at Neu-Buckow, Germany, the son of a country parson. It was from his father that young Heinrich first heard about ancient history. In his autobiography, he tells of the crucial event of his childhood: how, at the age of seven, he received for Christmas a copy of Jerrer's *Universal History*, with an illustration showing Troy in flames. Surely, reasoned the young Heinrich, walls so mighty could not have been destroyed? They must still be there . . .

His childhood was not happy. One of seven children, he was shattered by the death of his mother and by the scandal when his father took a maidservant as a mistress, and later when his father was accused of misappropriating church funds and dismissed (he was later exonerated). Heinrich and his father had many bitter arguments. At the age of fourteen, Heinrich became a grocer's assistant and had to work fourteen hours a day. Suffering from tuberculosis, he gave up his job and became a cabin boy on a boat sailing for South America; it was shipwrecked and he found himself eventually in Amsterdam. There he became a clerk, taught himself English and went on to learn nine foreign languages in six years. At the age of twenty-four, he was sent to Russia as the chief agent of an Amsterdam merchant. In 1850, he sailed for America to claim the estate of his brother Louis, who had died in California. He records in his diary that he called on the President of the United States, Zachary Taylor, and had an hour-and-a-half's conversation with him, meeting his family and being treated with great kindness. Then he went on to Sacramento, where he set up an office to buy gold dust from the miners, for the gold rush was at its height at that time. He amassed a fortune of $350,000 as a result. He noted in his diary that he was in San Francisco during the great fire of 1851. Back in Europe, he married a Russian beauty but she did not care for archaeology or travel and they eventually divorced. Schliemann visited Greece for the first time at the age of thirty-seven. Four years later, he was rich enough to realize the ambition of a lifetime and to become an archaeologist. He studied archaeology in Paris and travelled extensively in the Mediterranean area. In 1868 he visited Mycenae, in Greece — the home of Agamemnon — and propounded a startling theory that the royal tombs would be found within the ruined walls of the citadel, and not, as the Greek geographer

Pausanias stated, outside the walls. Soon after this he was awarded his doctorate by the University of Rostock, writing his thesis, according to his autobiography, in classical Greek.

An old friend, Archbishop Theoclitus Vimbos of Athens, helped him find a Greek wife. A sixteen-year-old schoolgirl, Sophia Engastromenos, was selected for him; her parents agreed, and the couple were married. Her parents were much impressed by his tales, particularly the story about the fire of San Francisco.

Schliemann was convinced that Troy really existed and that it was no legend, as many scholars believed. Those scholars who accepted the existence of Troy — ancient Ilion — thought that it was situated three hours from the sea near Bunarbashi, on the Balidagh, in a mountain fastness. On the evidence of Homer, Schliemann disagreed — Homer's heroes had ridden between Troy and the coast several times a day. He decided that the site of Troy was probably a mound at a place called Hissarlik, an hour from the sea. He obtained permission from the Turkish authorities to dig there and started in 1871, with a gang of eighty men.

It must be admitted that, as an archaeologist, Schliemann does not rate very highly. His method was as subtle as a bulldozer. He simply ordered his men to cut a deep trench through the mound. He soon discovered that the mound contained several cities, one on top of the other. Convinced that ancient Troy must be the lowest, he ordered his workmen to dig straight down to it, destroying all the ruins above, including those of the city archaeologists now know to be the Troy of Homer. The city Schliemann thought was the Troy of King Priam was in reality many centuries earlier.

In the following year, Schliemann's workmen sliced the top off the mound. Many discoveries came to light, but so far, there was no sign of the gold that Homer talked about. At least he found structures he identified as the royal palace, the wall of the gods, and the ramp leading to the Scaean Gate.

By the spring of 1883 he was becoming worried; he had still found no gold and he had agreed to end the excavations in June. Then, one day in May he thought he glimpsed a copper vessel through a hole in a wall. What followed has been told in breathless detail by more than twenty biographers of Schliemann. Afraid that his workmen would make off with part of his find, he waited until they were eating, then asked Sophia to help him remove the "treasure". Indifferent to his danger, for the wall above was made of loose masonry, he tore out the stones, aided by a large knife and, piece by piece, handed the marvellous gold objects – drinking vessels and jewellery – to his wife, who wrapped them in her shawl. Later, behind closed doors, Sophie was dressed in the jewels of Helen of Troy – Schliemann was later to take a photograph of her draped in the gold ornaments. In June he returned to Athens and finally announced his discovery of the treasure. It made him world famous. He was later to excavate Mycenae, where his guess about the situation of the tombs proved correct. He died in 1890, at the age of sixty-eight. Sophia survived him by forty years.

That is the story of Heinrich Schliemann, and it has been retold many times. Guides at Hissarlik still show fascinated tourists the spot where Schliemann discovered the treasure of Priam, only a few weeks before he was due to leave Troy for ever.

In 1972 William Calder, Professor of Classics at the University of Colorado, was asked to go to Schliemann's birthplace, Neu-Buckow, to give a lecture on the hundred-and-fiftieth anniversary of his birth. Studying the various biographies of the great man, he realized that about 90 per cent of their material came from Schliemann himself. As soon as he began to check source material, he discovered that Schliemann was rather less trustworthy than his admirers had assumed. Checking at the University of Rostock, Calder discovered that the doctoral thesis was not, as Schliemann had declared, written in classical Greek; it only had a short section in classical Greek and this was atrocious. Calder checked on the story about calling on the President of the United States and being kindly received; the reception at which Schliemann claimed he was presented to six hundred guests would certainly be mentioned in Washington newspapers. There was nothing whatever — Schliemann had invented it.

Calder's lecture about these saddening discoveries was read by David Trail, a classics professor at the University of California. In San Francisco, he was able to check the records of the bankers who had stored the gold dust that Schliemann had bought from the miners in Sacramento and found suggestions that Schliemann had systematically cheated them by sending them short-weight consignments. Checking Schliemann's account of the great fire of San Francisco, Trail discovered that Schliemann had quoted the wrong date — he gave it as 4 June 1851 when it had taken place on 4 May. Schliemann's papers are stored in Athens, and Trail checked the diary. The page with the account of the fire proved to have been glued in later. The page preceding it has an entry in Spanish, which continues on the following page. The account proved to have been culled from newspapers of the time.

Calder's opinion was that Schliemann was a pathological liar — a liar so convinced of his own romances that a lie-detector test would probably have indicated he was telling the truth. Even the story about seeing the pictures of Troy in a book he was given for Christmas proved to be an invention, fabricated later for Schliemann's book *Ilion*.

The diaries also revealed that there were doubts about the finding of the treasure. There was no entry for the discovery of the treasure; he speaks about it for the first time in an entry dated 17 June. In the published account, this entry is datelined from Troy. In the diary, "Athens" has been crossed out and "Troy" substituted. An entry that was a draft-account of the discovery for his German publishers fails to describe the treasure, with the exception of one gold cup, noted as having large handles and being shaped like a champagne glass, with a rounded bottom (the shape we would now describe as a hock glass). There is no such vessel among the treasure. The nearest to it is a kind of gold sauce boat with handles and the descriptions do not correspond. But Schliemann had unearthed many terracotta vessels that looked exactly like the "champagne glass" he described. It seems that he simply invented the item in order to give his publisher a foretaste of the treasure.

Further investigation revealed that Sophia was not present at the time Schliemann claims he found the treasure. She was in mourning for her father in Athens and did not return to Troy. And although excavations continued for two weeks after Schliemann claimed to have found the treasure – giving him plenty of time to describe it – there is nevertheless not a single description in his diary.

Foremost American author William Faulkner was virtually a pathological liar. "You never knew when he was telling the truth" said his cousin. When he came back from World War I in 1918, he was wearing an officer's uniform, and walked with a limp, which he claimed had been caused in a plane crash in France. In fact, he had been a private in the Canadian Royal Air Force (in which he impersonated an Englishman) for less than six months, had never flown a plane and had not been out of the United States.

The inference is that he did not find any treasure – at least, not in the manner he described.

But where did the treasure come from? Trail's conclusion was that the "treasure" was already back in Athens at the time Schliemann claims he discovered it. He was obliged by contract to share anything he found with the owners of the site, a Pasha and an American named Frank Calvert. What almost certainly happened is that Schliemann systematically cheated them, claiming he had found nothing, and smuggling his finds back to Athens – his letters often refer to objects that he failed to show to Calvert. In March, before the "finding" of the treasure, a letter mentions sixty gold rings – precisely the number of rings in the treasure.

That Schliemann found something is proved by the testimony of his trusted overseer, Nicolaos Yannakis, who later told an English antiquarian, William Borlase, that he had been with Schliemann at the time of the find and not Sophia. And the find contained no gold or jewellery – only a quantity of bronze objects, found in a stone enclosure outside the city wall.

So why did Schliemann do it? Psychoanalysts who have considered the problem have talked about his relationship with his father – the admiration combined with fear and dislike that compelled him to seek fame so that he could finally feel he had outstripped his father. This may or may not be true. All that is certain is that Schliemann craved fame and applause – his lie about the meeting with the President reveals the desire to impress. "We all bid for admiration with no intention of earning it," says Shaw. In his own devious way, Schliemann set out to earn it. He wanted to believe that he had found Homer's Troy; to complete the triumph he needed to find King Priam's treasure. And if the treasure did not exist, then it had to be made to exist. Only in this way could Schliemann achieve the kind of celebrity he craved.

But although these revelations reveal Schliemann as a

crook and a liar, they leave one part of his reputation untouched: that strange, intuitive genius that led him to dig in exactly the right place, first at Hissarlik and later at Mycenae. He may have been a confidence man, but he was still, in spite of everything, "the creator of prehistoric Greek archaeology".

Oscar Wilde – "One must seek out what is most tragic"

Oscar Wilde's father, Sir William Wilde, was a constant subject of Dublin gossip and scandal. Known as "the Wilde knight", he was reputed to be the father of many illegitimate children – Bernard Shaw said he had a child in every farmhouse. In 1864 (when Oscar was ten), a libel case against his wife, Lady Jane Francesca Wilde, turned into a trial of Sir William, a leading physician, on a charge of raping a female patient.

Lady Jane had written a furious letter to a Dr Travers, Professor of Medical Jurisprudence at Trinity College, accusing his daughter of blackmailing Sir William and disseminating a pamphlet accusing him of "an intrigue" with her. The daughter, Miss Mary Josephine Travers, decided to sue; she wanted £2,000 damages.

When the case came up on 12 December 1864, the prosecution lost no time in informing the jury that "the particulars . . . are of so shocking a description that I wish to God it had devolved upon some other counsel to present them . . ." Having cured Miss Travers of ear trouble, Sir William had lent her books and money, bought her bonnets and dresses, taken her to lectures and exhibitions, and finally raped her in his consulting room. (One lady fainted and had to be carried out of the courtroom.) She had gone to him to be treated for a burn on her neck and in the course of the treatment had fainted. She had awakened to realize that, alas, she was no longer a maid. Sir William had urged her to keep this quiet. Miss Travers had gone to Lady Wilde to complain but had been treated with scorn. She had attempted suicide with a dose of laudanum (opium) but had recovered. To redress her wrongs, she had printed the pamphlet accusing Sir William of taking advantage of her. When Miss Travers was called to the witness box, the judge told the ladies in the gallery that any who wished to do so might leave; no one did. Then the prosecution asked the question, "When you were unconscious was your person − er − violated?" and Miss Travers replied, "It was."

But the cross-examination was damaging. Why, Miss Travers was asked, did she accuse Sir William of violating her after administering chloroform? Miss Travers agreed that it had not happened like that but could give no excuse for printing a false version. Then Sergeant Sullivan, in Sir William's defence, went in for the kill. Had the alleged assault happened on other occasions? Blushing, Miss Travers admitted that it had. She explained that Sir William had led up to it with "rudeness and roughness". But the jury must have found it a little odd that a girl who had been raped while unconscious should give the rapist the opportunity to do it several times more − even with rudeness and roughness. The jury returned to say that they found Lady Wilde's letter libellous, which implied that her husband was guilty, but they awarded Miss Travers only one farthing in damages. The Wildes had to pay the considerable costs. Oscar should have learned from the example of Miss Travers that it can be dangerous to accuse someone of libel; it can lead to embarrassing counterclaims.

Oscar Wilde was born on 16 October 1854. At seventeen he won a scholarship to Trinity College, Dublin. There he came under the influence of the remarkable Professor of Ancient History, the Reverend John Pentland Mahaffy. It was from Mahaffy that Wilde picked up his passionate love of the classics, particularly those of ancient Greece. At this time, Wilde's sexual inclinations were basically heterosexual, with a mild touch of ambivalence, such as may also be noted in Lord Byron. And, as with Byron, his intellectual and emotional appreciation of Mediterranean pederasty laid the foundations for his later development.

At Trinity, and later at Oxford, Wilde was brilliant rather than hardworking. He had the typical charm of those born under Libra. At Oxford he came under the influence of John Ruskin, who taught him to appreciate painting and architecture, and Walter Pater, who taught that the basic aim of life is to live with "a hard, gem-like flame" and who revived Victor Cousin's phrase "Art for art's sake". Pater confirmed Wilde in that intellectual elitism he had picked up from Mahaffy, the feeling that the true aristocrats of this world are the men of brilliance and imagination. And when, at the age of twenty-three, he accompanied Mahaffy on a tour of Greece, the experience confirmed his conviction that beauty is the only ultimate value.

In his last year at Oxford, Wilde wrote to a friend: "I'll be famous, and if not famous, I'll be notorious." And when he went to join his mother in London — his father had died — he decided to become both at once. His elder brother Willie, who had become a journalist, introduced him to editors, and Wilde published some poems. He fell in love with the famous beauty Lily Langtry, mistress of the Prince of Wales, and wrote her a number of poems. When a volume of verse failed to bring him fame, he announced that a revolution in dress was more important than a revolution in morals, and began to call attention to himself with a velvet coat edged with braid, knee breeches and black silk stockings. He was one of the first great modern experts in the art of self-publicity. By 1880, he was being regularly satirized in *Punch*. In the following years, W.S. Gilbert portrayed him in *Patience* as the mediocre poet Bunthorne. Gilbert no doubt thought he was being cruel but Wilde was delighted with the notoriety it brought him. This led to a request to go on a lecture tour of America. Wilde arrived in New York with the typical comment, "I have nothing to declare but my genius." He was not particularly fond of America. Later, when he heard that Rossetti had given someone the money to go to America he commented, "Of course, if one had enough money to go to America, one wouldn't go."

In 1833, after a lecture tour of Scotland, he announced his engagement to Constance Lloyd, daughter of an Irish barrister, a beautiful and sweet-natured girl. They were deeply in love and on the morning after his wedding night, Wilde strolled in Paris with his friend Robert Sherard and described his sexual pleasures with embarrassing detail. Two sons were born of the marriage.

It was about two years after his marriage that Wilde made a shattering discovery. At Oxford he had contracted syphilis from a prostitute and had been "cured" with mercury treatment (which had discoloured his teeth). Now he learned that the spirochetes were still in his bloodstream. With modern treatment he would have been cured in a weekend. As it was, he felt that he had to give up sex with Constance. At about this time he met a seventeen-year-old youth named Robert ("Robbie") Ross, who was amusing, cultivated and amiable. Ross later claimed that he was the first male Wilde had been to bed with.

Success was slow in arriving; early plays like *Vera, or the Nihilists* and *The Duchess of Padua* failed to make an impression. He was literary critic for the *Pall Mall Gazette*, and he became the editor of a magazine called *The Lady's World* (renamed *Woman's World*). He wrote short stories, children's stories, poems and essays. Finally, in 1891, when he was thirty-seven, *The Picture of Dorian Gray* appeared and caused a degree of public outrage that he must have found highly satisfying. In the following year, *Lady Windermere's Fan* went on at the St James's Theatre and finally made Wilde rich as well as famous.

Scandals

French car tycoon Andre Citroen liked to think big. During the Paris Exposition in 1922 he had an airplane spell out his name in white smoke above the fair, while Citroen cars all over the city gave citizens rides to the fair. Many of his fellow French citizens were outraged by his display, but when his sales rocketed, Citroen quickly came up with another gimmick – he had his name it up on the Eiffel Tower with 25,000 electric bulbs. Eventually however, Citroen spent all his money, mainly on women and gambling and died flat broke. He used to plan on losing at the gaming tables for publicity reasons – up to 13,000 francs at a time.

In the year of *Dorian Gray*, Wilde met a handsome young aristocrat of twenty-two, Lord Alfred Douglas, son of the Marquess of Queensberry (responsible for the Queensberry Rules in boxing). Soon they were inseparable, dining in expensive restaurants, spending weekends at country houses, attending art exhibitions and first nights. Inevitably, they slept together, although Douglas later insisted that there was no sodomy – only mutual masturbation and a certain amount of oral sex. "Bosie" (as Wilde called Lord Alfred) was himself a pederast and preferred boys to older men. The French novelist André Gide has described how Wilde and Douglas were responsible for his own downfall. For years he had been struggling against his homosexuality. In Algiers, he discovered that Wilde and Douglas were staying in the same hotel – he had met Wilde in Paris. Before they set out for the evening, Douglas remarked to Gide, "I hope you are like me. I have a horror of women. I only like boys." Wilde told the "vile procurer who came to pilot us through the town" that he wanted to see some Arab boys and added "as beautiful as bronze statues". But a brawl broke out in the café the procurer took them to and they went home disappointed. Soon after, Douglas went off to Blidah, where he was hoping to buy an Arab boy from his family (in fact, the boy ran away with a woman). Wilde took Gide out for another evening in the Casbah, and in a little café, a beautiful Arab youth came and played on a flute for them. Then Wilde led Gide outside and whispered in his ear, "Dear, would you like the little musician?" and Gide, his voice choking, answered, "Yes." Later, the youth came to a hotel room and Gide wrote: "My joy was unbounded, and I cannot imagine it greater even if love had been added."

Back in London, Wilde met Alfred Taylor, an upper-class young man who had spent his way through a fortune. Taylor was a homosexual who liked to dress as a woman; he burned incense in his dimly lit apartment and spent his days picking up young men — many of them telegraph boys of the kind who figured in the Cleveland Street scandal — and taking them back to his room for sex. The first youth Taylor picked up for Wilde was a twenty-year-old named Sidney Mavor — known in his own circle as Jenny. The following evening, Wilde took Taylor, Douglas and "Jenny" to dinner at Kettner's and afterwards Wilde and Mavor went to a hotel room together. It emerged later that Wilde's idea of sex was to have the boy seated on his knee, while he fondled his genitals and occasionally indulged in oral sex. Wilde would tell them to imagine they were women and that he was their lover, which suggests that his role was fundamentally masculine and dominant. He disliked obviously feminine youths — he commented once that having sex with coarse, masculine types gave him a feeling of "dining with panthers". His appetite seems to have been enormous — he told Beardsley once that he had had five messenger boys in one evening and had kissed them all over their bodies. "They were all dirty and appealed to me for that reason."

Some time in 1893, Douglas gave a suit of clothes to an unemployed clerk, who found in the pockets a number of letters from Wilde. The result was an attempt to blackmail Wilde. "A very curious construction can be put on that letter," said the blackmailer, to which Wilde replied, "Art is rarely intelligible to the criminal classes." When the blackmailer said he could get £60 for the letter from a certain man, Wilde advised him to go and sell it immediately. The astonished blackmailer relented and gave Wilde the letter back for nothing — an example of Wilde's extraordinary charm, which was based upon a fundamental kindliness.

Unfortunately, a copy of the letter fell into the hands of the Marquess of Queensberry who was particularly outraged by the sentence: "it is a marvel that those rose-red lips of yours should have been made no less for music of song than for the madness of kisses." Queensberry was an eccentric Scottish aristocrat — in *The Trial of Oscar Wilde* Montgomery Hyde calls him "arrogant, vain, conceited and ill tempered", and says that he was probably mentally unbalanced. One day when Queensberry saw Wilde and his son dining together at the Café Royal, he allowed himself to be persuaded to join them, and was dazzled by Wilde's charm, and told "Bosie" afterwards that he could understand why he loved him. The "rose-red lips" letter seems to have changed his mind and he wrote a furious letter ordering Douglas never to see Wilde again. Douglas replied with a telegram: "What a funny little man you are." Queensberry began to haunt the restaurants where Wilde and Douglas dined, threatening to thrash Wilde. One afternoon, the Marquess came to Wilde's house to order him to stop seeing his son. Wilde ordered him, and his bodyguard, out. Queensberry continued to persecute Wilde. He tried to get into the theatre on the first night of *The Importance of Being Earnest*, but was kept out by police. On 18 February 1895, he left his card at Wilde's club, the Albemarle, with a note written on it: "To Oscar Wilde, posing as a sodomite" [sic]. When he received it two weeks later, Wilde decided to sue. He went to see a solicitor, Charles Humphries, and assured him that the accusation of being a sodomite was untrue. (He may well have felt he was being honest – he was not, as we know, inclined to sodomy.) Humphries agreed to prosecute.

The first trial proved a disaster for Wilde. His old schoolfellow Edward Carson was defending. Wilde was brilliant and amusing in the witness box but when Carson declared in court that he would prove that Wilde brought boys to the Savoy Hotel, it was obvious that Queensberry had done his homework – or paid private detectives to do it – and the prosecution realized it would have to withdraw or suffer defeat. The Marquess was acquitted.

Now Wilde's friends begged him to flee the country. Homosexuality was a criminal offence. Wilde refused and there was undoubtedly a touch of masochism in his refusal. In fact, he seemed to identify himself with Christ and to believe that he had to live out a tragic destiny. ("One must always seek what is most tragic", Wilde had told Gide.) On the day the Marquess was acquitted, a warrant was issued for Wilde's arrest, on a charge of committing acts of indecency with various male persons. Taylor, who had refused to betray Wilde, was also charged with him. This, Montgomery Hyde insists, was unfair to Wilde, since the case against Taylor was a great deal stronger than that against Wilde. The second trial lasted from 6 April to 19 April 1895. The judge's summing up was in Wilde's favour – at least, he urged the jury to take into account every possible doubt of Wilde's guilt. The jury failed to reach an agreement. For the next three weeks Wilde was out on bail.

The third trial began on 20 May 1895, and this time, Taylor was tried separately. He was soon found guilty of indecent acts with males. Then Wilde stepped into the dock.

Scandals

Again, a succession of working-class young men described being taken back to Wilde's room. Sodomy sometimes took place; more often, mutual masturbation and fellatio. Wilde was again brilliant and amusing in the box but seldom convincing. Finally, as everyone by now expected, Wilde was found guilty on every count but one. He and Taylor were sentenced to two years' imprisonment with hard labour.

Wilde was taken to Reading jail. Standing around on the station platform he remarked to the guard, "If this is the way Her Majesty treats her prisoners, she doesn't deserve to have any." But the old sparkle had gone. The experience of prison almost drove Wilde insane. He wallowed in self-pity and wrote a long letter — in fact, a short book — to Alfred Douglas, accusing him of his ruin. It was later published, in an expurgated version, as *De Profundis*. His hard labour consisted in picking oakum (that is unpicking old ropes for caulking boats). He served every day of his sentence and was finally released on 19 May 1897.

The poet Algernon Charles Swinburne scandalized the Victorians by writing poetry that was frankly sensuous. But he himself had little or no interest in normal sex; he was obsessed by flogging, and regularly attended a brothel in St John's wood to be flogged by prostitutes dressed up as governesses. The American actress Ada Mencken accepted a fee of £10 to seduce him, from his friend Rossetti, but returned the money with a confession of failure; she said she had been unable to persuade Swinburne that biting was no substitute for intercourse.

The desire to write had vanished. "Something is killed in me", he told Robbie Ross. Constance Wilde died in a nursing home in Genoa after an operation to correct a spinal injury, soon after reading Wilde's long poem *The Ballad of Reading Gaol*. Wilde went to Dieppe, where he bumped into the poet Ernest Dowson, who persuaded him to go to a brothel. Wilde did not enjoy it. "The first in these ten years — and it will be the last," he told Dowson. "It was like cold mutton." He lived in Paris under the name of Sebastian Melmoth — borrowing the name from the Gothic novel *Melmoth the Wanderer* by Maturin — and died in poverty in a cheap hotel on the Left Bank on 30 November 1900, telling a friend who came to see him, "I am dying beyond my means."

Ivor Novello – The Red Rolls-Royce Scandal

In April 1944, a year before the end of World War II, newspapers all over England carried headlines: Famous Actor Jailed For Petrol Offence. Ivor Novello, Britain's most famous matinée idol, had been sentenced to two months' imprisonment for an offence that amounted to fraud.

Ivor Novello was born David Ivor Davies in Cardiff, Wales, the son of an accountant and a music teacher. He was taught singing by his mother and proved to be brilliantly gifted. At the age of ten he took first prize for singing at a National Eisteddfod and his soprano voice won him a singing scholarship to Magdalen College, Oxford. He wanted to become a composer and conductor. His first song was published when he was sixteen, and was performed – without much success — at the Royal Albert Hall in London with Novello as accompanist. His first successful song, "The Little Damozel", appeared when he was seventeen, and was soon being sung by every soprano in the country. At this time, he also moved to London, supported by a modest income from his songs. He became famous at twenty-one, in 1914, with the song "Keep the Home Fires Burning", which became almost a second national anthem during World War I. The singer, John McCormick, earned £20,000 from his recording of this song alone.

During the war Novello served in the Royal Naval Air Service but after two crashes he was transferred to the Air Ministry. There, in 1916, he wrote half the music for a show called *Theodore and Co.* produced by the actor George Grossmith. His fellow composer was Jerome Kern. The show ran for eighteen months at the Gaiety.

After the war, Novello was asked if he would act in a film *The Call of the Blood* which was filmed in Rome. It was an immense success. Novello had exactly the right kind of romantic good looks for a silent screen star and acting ability was hardly required — although he had his share of that too. In the 1920s he was a film star, an actor-manager, a composer and a playwright. People argued whether he or John Barrymore had "the world's most handsome profile". He starred in Hitchcock's "first true film" *The Lodger* in 1926 — it has become a classic of the silent cinema. But it was in 1935 that he achieved a new dimension of fame with *Glamorous Night*, a combination of drama and musical with lavish spectacle. His formula was escapist romance and it was exactly what the audiences of the 1930s craved. *Careless Rapture* (1936) and *The Dancing Years* (1939) repeated the success. When World War II broke out in 1939, he had a luxurious flat in the Aldwych and a country home near Maidenhead. He was driven around in a red Rolls-Royce inscribed with his initials in black.

As the petrol shortage increased, it became increasingly difficult for Novello to travel from London to his country home for the weekend. His secretary wrote to the Regional Transport Commissioner's office to request extra petrol for him to drive to Maidenhead on the grounds that he needed to spend the weekends there writing his plays. The application was twice turned down. Just before Christmas 1942, Novello went into his dressing room where there was a crowd of admirers and asked despondently, "Anyone want a Rolls? Mine's no good to me."

Among the admirers in the room was a dumpy, middle-aged woman who had adored Novello from afar for years and gradually managed to get herself accepted among his retinue. He knew her as Grace Walton but her real name was Dora Constable. She now told Novello that she might be able to solve his problem. She was, she said, the secretary of the managing director of a firm with an office at Reading. She suggested that she might be able to apply for a special licence if the car was transferred to her firm for "war work". All this was arranged by Novello's secretary. The car was formally transferred into the firm's name; the firm even took over the insurance policy. Then Dora Constable wrote to the Regional Transport Commissioner to ask for a licence to "facilitate speedier transport by the managing director and his staff between our many works and factories". A few weeks later she collected the permit and handed it to Novello. He was effusively grateful and gave her a pair of earrings that had belonged to his mother, who had recently died.

Whether the firm actually made use of the initialled Rolls-Royce is not clear. Novello's biographer Peter Noble implies that it did, and that Novello then simply used the car "from time to time" to take him from London to Maidenhead. But if this is so, then it is difficult to see why the firm was shocked to discover that it was supposed to be the owner of Ivor Novello's Rolls-Royce. For this is what happened in October 1943, almost two years after Novello had received his permit. The managing director of the firm rang Novello and asked him to come to his office. On arrival, he learned that his admirer was not called Grace

Ivor Novello as the mysterious stranger in the film "The Lodger"

Walton but Dora Constable, and that she was not the managing director's secretary but a filing clerk. The firm knew nothing whatever about the deal with the Rolls-Royce.

Novello realized that he could be in serious trouble. Not long before, the bandleader Jack Hylton had been fined £155 and sentenced to two weeks in jail for a similar petrol-rationing offence. (In the event the jail sentence was quashed.)

Novello decided against a cover-up – he felt it was not his fault. He informed the authorities what had happened and so did the firm. An inspector from the Fuel Ministry came to see him and Novello rather ungallantly put all the blame on Dora Constable, saying it was her idea and that he had no suspicion that he was doing anything illegal. This, of course, was nonsense; he knew he was using a false permit for his petrol. His waspishness backfired. When his remarks were repeated to Dora Constable, she replied indignantly that Novello was being unfair. He had known exactly what he was doing and even made various suggestions about the transfer. "He was willing to do anything crooked as long as he had the use of the car."

With a statement like that, the authorities had to act. On 24 March 1944, Novello was summoned to appear at Bow Street Court. He went to pieces and protested, "The suggestion of my conspiring with a person of this woman's type is repugnant." But it was too late. On 24 April 1944, he stood in the dock at Bow Street alongside Dora Constable. His self-pitying remarks were quoted to the magistrate. The managing director of the firm went into the witness box and admitted, "Novello was deceived as completely as I was."

Novello gave one of his worst performances in the witness box. He was muddled and panic-stricken, and he gave the unfortunate impression that he was trying to unload the blame on to Dora Constable. The judge was an old-fashioned gentleman and there can be no doubt that Novello's attempt to dodge the blame revolted him. Dora Constable was fined £50 with £25 costs. Novello was fined £100. But, added Mr Justice McKenna, "that would obviously be no punishment for a man like you, so I sentence you to eight weeks' imprisonment." Novello was granted bail, pending an appeal. Shattered and stricken, he staggered from the court.

Two months later, on 16 May 1944, the appeal was heard at the London Sessions courthouse. The Chairman of the appeals committee was Mr Eustace Fulton who had quashed Jack Hylton's prison sentence. This time he was not in such a lenient mood. When Novello's secretary Fred Allen said that he had no suspicion there was anything wrong about the car transaction, "otherwise I wouldn't have touched the damn thing", Fulton rebuked him for the use of "damn". Allen stammered nervously and Fulton snapped, "Oh, get on!" The defending solicitor said, "I am sorry your Lordship shows signs of impatience." The judge snorted, "I have shown every patience." It did not bode well for Novello. And in spite of some distinguished character witnesses – Sir Lewis Casson, Dame Sybil Thorndike, Sir Edward Marsh – the most Fulton would concede was that Novello's sentence was perhaps too long and halved it to four weeks. As Novello left the court he turned and flung open his arms "in a gesture of infinite despair".

Novello was not a good prisoner. Although the authorities at Wormwood Scrubs leaned over backwards to treat him kindly – he was placed in charge of the prison choir – he almost went insane with despair and he plunged into extravagant self-pity. When he was released on 13 June 1944 he looked thin and haggard. A week later, he returned to the stage in *The Dancing Years* and was cheered by a sympathetic audience who delayed the start of the show by ten minutes. His biographer Peter Noble is nevertheless convinced that the jail sentence should be regarded as a tragedy. Novello died seven years later of a heart attack at the age of fifty-eight. He was to write three more successes after his prison sentence: *Perchance to Dream, King's Rhapsody* and *Gay's the Word*. Noble believes the sentence shortened his life. In *Scales of Justice*, Fenton Bresler speculates that the prison sentence also cost Novello the knighthood that crowned the careers of most of his successful theatrical contemporaries.

Yet for the objective observer, it is hard to feel too much pity for Novello. His own behaviour was almost certainly responsible for the prison sentence. The obvious self-pity, the attempt to lay the blame on his admirer, who showed altogether more dignity when she decided not to testify, undoubtedly produced a mood of impatience in both judges. They probably felt that he was a spoiled brat who deserved a rap on the knuckles. Novello's real problem was that his life had been an almost unbroken run of success and until he was middle aged he always had his adored mother to give him approval and moral support. The result was that he never really grew up. And, like a certain type of homosexual, he was prone to self-pity and self-dramatization. He once told Peter Noble, "I have a suspicion that Fate has a sense of humour, and a rather malicious one. Fate says, 'Ah, that boy's had a success. He is getting a bit above himself. Now for a few slips!'" A little more of this attitude might have averted the prison sentence or at least made it more bearable.

"Professor" C.E.M. Joad – The Rail-Ticket Scandal

When "Professor" Joad was caught out trying to dodge paying his rail fare in January 1948, he was a famous public figure, a writer and broadcaster whose favourite expression

"It depends what you mean by . . ." had become a popular catch-phrase. The incident of the rail ticket brought his career to a premature close.

Cyril Edward Mitchinson Joad was born in Durham on 12 August 1891, the son of a school inspector. He was educated at Blundell's, the famous public school, and at Balliol College, Oxford. At twenty-three he was awarded the John Locke scholarship in mental philosophy and on coming down from Oxford, he became a civil servant in the Board of Trade. He later declared that he used his sixteen years as a civil servant mainly to write his books. By 1924, his *Introduction to Modern Philosophy* had underneath his name: "Author of *Essays in Common Sense Philosophy*, *Common Sense Ethics*, *Common Sense Theology*, etc." In his book on Shaw, Joad tells how he came to Oxford in 1910 and read simultaneously Wells's *Tono Bungay* and Shaw's *Candida*, and of the "heady exhilaration" of this "intoxicating intellectual brew". A meeting with Shaw soon after that turned him into a "Shaw-worshipper". Joad himself had something in common both with Shaw and Wells: like Shaw, he was an incorrigible "performer" who loved to propagate the myth of himself – even his titles reveal his obsessive self-preoccupation: *The Book of Joad*, *The Testament of Joad*, *The Pleasure of Being Oneself*; like Wells, he was an incurable philanderer. He once said that at the age of eleven he thought all women were solid from the waist down; his discovery that they were, so to speak, accessible seems to have resulted in a lifelong desire to prove that there were no exceptions to the rule. He also said once that he had no interest in speaking with a woman unless she was willing to sleep with him. He called all his mistresses Maureen, in case he made a slip of the tongue in addressing them. His wife, whom he married in 1915, seemed to accept his *affaires*.

Joad was one of the great popularizers; his *Guide to Philosophy* (1936) was as influential, in its way, as Wells's

Outline of History or Hogben's *Mathematics for the Million*. But Joad was by no means an intellectual lightweight; his *Matter, Life and Value* (1929) is a brilliant and original exposition of the philosophy of "vitalism". He believed firmly in the reality of objective values and had no sympathy with the tendency of the logical positivists to dismiss metaphysics. He was, in his way, a religious man. But he was inclined to model himself on Shaw and to waste a great deal of his time in controversy, to the detriment of his serious work. From the age of thirty-nine, he became head of the department of philosophy at Birkbeck College, London; but he was never, strictly speaking, a "professor".

In 1941, the British Broadcasting Corporation started a programme called "The Brains Trust", broadcast on its "Forces" wavelength. It was so popular that it was soon repeated on the Home Service. Soon it had become — together with Tommy Handley's comedy show ITMA — one of the most successful programmes of the war years. Joad had a rather precise, high-pitched voice, and sounded exactly like the popular idea of a university professor. *Punch* carried a cartoon of him saying to a waiter: "It all depends on what you mean by (a) thick, and (b) clear." He became so popular that police had to escort him through the crowds at public meetings, and the Ministry of Food launched a dish called "Joad-in-the-Hole". He loved his notoriety. "He was an immensely vain individual", his BBC producer told Fenton Bresler, who devoted a chapter to Joad in his book *Scales of Justice*. The least suggestion of a snub could throw him into a towering rage but a soft answer — particularly if it was mixed with a judicious dose of flattery — had him cooing like a dove. He was not much liked at the BBC, partly because of a pathological meanness that made him dodge paying for his round of drinks whenever possible.

At 10.50 on the morning of 5 January 1948, Joad boarded the Atlantic Coast Express at Paddington, bound for Exeter in Devon; his secretary was with him. Both

"Professor" C.E.M. Joad

booked for the second sitting at lunch. When the ticket collector came to their table at lunch, his secretary held out her ticket but Joad explained: "I haven't got one. I was late and the collector let me through. I got on at Salisbury." The ticket collector gave him a return from Exeter to Salisbury. But the dining car attendant, who overheard the exchange, told the collector that there was something odd going on; Joad and his secretary had booked for lunch before the train reached Salisbury. The inspector went back to question Joad, who persisted in saying that he had boarded at Salisbury. It was only when the train stopped at Exeter

---

Ernst Roehm – the leader of the two and a half million strong Brown Shirt Storm Troopers, the street-fighting arm of the Nazi Party – was a brutal, working-class demagogue with undisguised homosexual tendencies, but had been with Hitler from the beginning and was one of his closest colleagues. The aristocratic Prussian Military High Command loathed him instinctively and wanted him destroyed at any cost. One general later said of the Brown Shirts, "[Germany's] rearmament was too serious and difficult a business to permit the participation of peculators, drunkards and homosexuals."

Hitler also felt Roehm was becoming too powerful. In the early morning of 30th June, 1934, he ordered the entire Brown Shirt Command arrested for treason. Roehm and many of his colleagues were found in the Hanslbaur Hotel at Weissee, most asleep in one another's beds or with teenage boys. All were taken to the yard and shot.

---

that Joad admitted: "I made a mistake. I did come from Paddington . . ." He had indeed made a mistake to admit his guilt. If Joad had kept silent, he would undoubtedly have heard the last of it. He made a further mistake by writing to the railway authorities and explaining that the problem had been a "misunderstanding".

What decided the authorities to take Joad to court was undoubtedly their discovery that this was not the first time and that he had made a habit of travelling without a ticket for years. On 12 April 1948, counsel on his behalf pleaded guilty at the Tower Bridge magistrates' court to "unlawfully travelling on the railway without having previously paid his fare and with intent to avoid payment." Joad was fined £2, with 25 guineas costs. That evening a newspaper carried the headline: Joad Fined For Common Ticket Fraud. Joad had tried to save himself 17s. 1d. On the same evening, Joad was on "The Brains Trust" and seemed as jaunty and confident as ever. But in Parliament the following Friday, a Tory MP said, "In the last week a public figure was convicted for telling lies and defrauding the public and he was hired the same evening by the BBC to entertain people." On the evening of Joad's next scheduled appearance, he was dropped in favour of Commander King-Hall. He never again appeared on "The Brains Trust".

Joad continued to write books but he knew that, as a moral philosopher, his authority was gone. He became a practising Christian and wrote books about his new religious belief. In 1953, at the age of sixty-two, he died of cancer.

Why did Joad do it? When he was asked this question by the "Brains Trust" question master, Donald McCullough, he replied: "*Hubris*" — the Greek word for pride or conceit. Another motive was clearly his meanness. But his friend Hugh Schonfield, the Biblical scholar, has a different explanation. He told the present writer (CW) that Joad always had a need to "kick over the traces". Rebellion was a basic necessity of his nature — thumbing his nose at authority. So although he was "Britain's foremost philosopher" (as he claimed at the head of his newspaper column) and a famous public figure, there was a need to reassure himself that he was still a rebel at heart by small acts of antisocial defiance.

Chapter Five

Political Scandals

S candals of the political nature scream into the headlines when a politician has put himself (or herself) into an embarrassing position that leaves nothing to the imagination. President John Kennedy openly had numerous women attend to him, even though he was married, and didn't seem to worry, or care, what effect this would have on his political career. In 1906 Wilhelm Voigt impersonated a captain in the German army and "arrested" the mayor of a town, taking his cash box with all its money and then disappearing. The story caused great hilarity in Germany at the time.

Wilhelm Voigt –
"The Captain of Kopenick"

The story of the bogus "Captain of Kopenick" made all Kaiser Wilhelm's Germany rock with laughter. On the morning of 17 October 1906, a troop of ten soldiers, headed by a sergeant, was marching through Tegel (in Berlin). Suddenly, a man in a captain's uniform stepped in front of them and roared, "Halt!" The captain was a plump man with a drooping moustache, in his late fifties. He inspected the squad, then ordered the sergeant to accompany him to Kopenick, a dozen or so miles away, where he had official business at the town hall. Being Prussians, they obeyed without question. When they arrived at Kopenick, the captain gave them a mark each and told them to fall out for the midday meal. After their meal, he lined them up outside the town hall and set guards at the doors, ordering them to keep callers from entering. Then he marched the remaining seven men into the building, set some of them as guards on stairs and in corridors, and marched into the mayor's office. The captain informed the mayor that he was under arrest. Then he demanded to be shown the cash box with the municipal funds. It contained 4,000 marks which he confiscated, after carefully counting them.

The captain ordered his men to lead the prisoner away, while a soldier was told to requisition three vehicles. Into the first two of these, the soldiers and the mayor were ordered; their destination was a police station some fifteen miles away. The captain and the cash box entered the other cab. It was this cab that failed to arrive at the police station. It took more than two hours of confusion and mutual recriminations before it dawned on the police and the mayor that they were victims of a hoax.

The "captain" was an old lag named Wilhelm Voigt, who had spent twenty-seven of his fifty-seven years in jail. He had walked into a pawn shop, shortly after his release from his latest spell in prison, and purchased the second-hand captain's uniform. It is not clear whether the robbery was planned, or whether it was a spur of the moment decision as he saw the soldiers marching through Tegel.

The news of the comic-opera robbery spread round the world. Even the Kaiser is said to have roared with laughter when he heard about it and said, "Such a thing could only happen in Germany." From the description, it didn't take the police long to identify the captain as Voigt. While all the Berlin police searched for him, the city was flooded with picture postcards of the exploit showing the trembling mayor standing before the ferocious captain, while another showed Voigt winking and smoking a fat cigar. The newspaper *Berliner Tageblat* said that he ought to be rewarded, not punished, for teaching the Germans a lesson.

Voigt was arrested ten days later in his room in a Berlin slum. Most of the 4,000 marks were still unspent. He was sentenced to four years in jail but this was later reduced to twenty months – on the direct intervention of the Kaiser, it was whispered.

Voigt came out of prison in 1908 and discovered that a dramatist called Kalnberg had written a successful play called *The Captain of Kopenick*. Voigt requested, and received, a free seat for a performance of the play.

The case had political echoes. In 1910, Herr von Oldenburg-Januschau, a fire-eating right winger, defended Prussian militarism against the dangerous liberalism that seemed to be undermining the country. He declared, "It must always be possible for the German Emperor and King of Prussia to tell the nearest lieutenant: take ten men and close down the Reichstag (parliament)." This sentiment backfired as comedians all over Germany parodied the statement. After the exploit of Wilhelm Voigt, Prussian authoritarianism was no longer treated with quite the same respect.

President John F. Kennedy – All the President's Women

During his political career – spanning the late 1940s, the prudish fifties and the pre-hippy years of the sixties – John F. Kennedy pursued a sex-life that would make most of us dizzy to contemplate.

Protected and covered-up for by friends and colleagues, tactfully ignored by a more gentlemanly (not to say timorous) media, and almost unassailably popular with his supporters, he indulged himself with almost every attractive woman who showed willing – and there were plenty of those for the glamorous Jack Kennedy. Nobody has ever tried to put a figure to his conquests, but these must have been well into the upper hundreds.

In his book, *"Kennedy and His Women"*, Tony Sciacca

records numerous accounts of Kennedy's philandering from those close to him throughout his political career. Reading the anecdotes one soon forms an impression that Jack Kennedy must have viewed attractive women in the same light that a voracious reader might consider paperbacks. He clearly needed a continuous and ever-changing supply of lovers, yet he seems to have viewed sex more as a relaxing and necessary pastime than the driving force of his life.

However, this did not stop him from allowing his sex-drive to occasionally impinge on his political life. He often spent pleasant afternoons (when his wife Jackie was away) bathing naked in the Whitehouse swimming pool with whatever young lady or ladies he presently had attached to his entourage. Hassled presidential aides had a lively time stopping uninitiated ministers and diplomats wandering round to the pool to have a quick word with Mr President.

During the 1962 Nassau conference he shocked the British Prime Minister, Harold Macmillan, by offhandedly saying: "You know, I get very severe headaches if I go too long without a woman." He then excused himself and left with two attractive members of his personal staff, who up to then had seemed to fulfil no specific purpose. An hour later he returned alone, looking much refreshed. Smiling, he told the mildly indignant Prime Minister: "My headache's gone."

Life as a Kennedy Whitehouse staffer could be both hectic and demanding. The secret service men seconded to protect the President were given the additional duty of unobtrusively sneaking-in his girlfriends on demand. Presidential aides often had to rush about tidying-up the evidence of the President's visitors when Mrs Kennedy's pending arrival was unexpectedly announced. Possible hairpins were searched for in thick carpets, beds were rapidly remade and the odd female garment swiftly relocated.

On one occasion they were a bit lax in their efforts and

Scandals

Jackie Kennedy found a pair of women's panties stuffed in a pillow case. She calmly handed them to her husband saying, "Would you please shop around and see who these belong to? They're not my size."

It seems clear that Jackie knew about at least some of the other women, but aside from creating a slight distancing from her husband, she did not let it spoil her marriage. One must respect her fortitude; she not only had to put-up with the arduous life of the First Lady, but had also to contend with the fact that her husband was totally incapable of being faithful to her.

In contrast to contemporary politicians, Kennedy seems to have been totally unconcerned that his enemies might use his private life to wreck his career. In 1952, during his first campaign to enter the Senate, a photograph of Kennedy and a young lady lying naked on a sun drenched beach came into the hands of his Republican opponent, Henry Cabot Lodge. Instead of handing it straight to the media, Lodge had a copy of the photograph sent to Kennedy's campaign headquarters, where it caused quite a stir.

Kennedy's campaign strategists examined the photograph and despaired; it looked like the end of his electoral chances and possibly his entire political career. It was decided that Kennedy must be informed of the situation and several unhappy aides took the photograph to his office. One later said that Kennedy "just looked at the picture a long time and then told us about all the great times he had with the girl and how fond he'd been of her. He put it in his desk and told us not to worry about it." Lodge did not publish the photograph, perhaps merely hoping to shake his opponent's confidence, and Kennedy won the election easily.

Another example of Jack Kennedy's rakish attitude to women is related by a fellow congressman who attended an informal dinner party thrown by Kennedy at his Washington house in 1948. Also present were several of Kennedy's Navy friends from his war service days and an attractive red-head from an airline ticket office that Kennedy had casually asked along.

She noticed that he was not eating and asked him why. Kennedy replied: "How can I eat when all I'm thinking about is taking you upstairs?" She replied that she wasn't hungry either and they excused themselves and went upstairs.

Later they all went to the movies after which Kennedy packed his date off in a cab. As soon as she was gone he called another young lady. He said he had met her a few weeks before at Palm Beach, and had offered to show her the sights of Washington. They picked her up at her hotel and drove back to Kennedy's house. After a brandy the Congressman and his date tactfully left.

The next day the Congressman met Kennedy on Capitol Hill and asked how things had gone. Kennedy said he had a terrible time. His new date seems to have thought that "after one screw with Jack Kennedy she was going to marry him." She had finally stormed out at about two in the morning. "Then he turned and waved toward some real luscious woman sitting up in the House gallery. And he stage whispered to me: 'She's the one I spent the night with.' Jack wasn't bragging. To him, it was all very casual, something that a bachelor had coming to him . . . I tell you, I was awfully jealous of that man. The women seemed to be coming out of the woodwork . . ."

This playboyish detachment seems to have characterized Kennedy's dealings with women. Yet, despite the modern view of Don Juanism, his womanizing almost certainly did not spring from a contempt for the female sex. Even his detractors admit that he invariably behaved with courtesy and tact in his love affairs and, as can be seen above, he was at pains to avoid giving the impression that he wanted anything other than a casual commitment.

Scandals

Although most of Kennedy's affairs were short term – as little as a couple of hours in some cases – he also maintained a few longer lasting relationships – the most notorious perhaps being with the icon goddesses, Marilyn Monroe and Jayne Mansfield. His basic good nature was again illustrated by his conduct in these affairs. He would go to elaborate lengths to ensure that the lady was protected from difficulties while being almost cavalier with his own reputation.

At the beginning of World War II Kennedy was stationed in Washington, working in the ONI, the Office of Navy Intelligence. Captain Alan Kirk, director of the ONI, was an old family friend, and Jack's father, Joe Kennedy, – then Ambassador to Great Britain – had pulled strings to get his boy into a plum job. Yet by January 1942, Jack had been kicked-out of Naval Intelligence and sent to a minor desk job in South Carolina. The reason was one Inga Arvad, a gorgeous Danish journalist whom Adolf Hitler had once described as "a perfect Nordic beauty".

Inga had come from Europe with her pro-Nazi husband, had left him for a suspected pro-Nazi and had eventually ended-up working on *The Washington Times-Herald* on a society column, through which she met Jack. The FBI already saw her as a potential Mata-Hari and her involvement with a young intelligence officer in a key position decided them. They bugged her telephone and had her kept under surveillance.

Great pressure was placed on Jack, by the Navy and his father, to break with Inga, but he remained intransigent. His lover was not, he insisted, a Nazi spy. Eventually he pulled enough strings to receive an interview with FBI director J. Edgar Hoover himself. Hoover was forced to admit that there was absolutely no evidence against Inga and apologized on behalf of the Bureau. Jack Kennedy at the age of twenty-five, with the mere rank of Navy Ensign, had faced down one of the most powerful men in the country to protect the reputation of his lover.

J. Edgar Hoover must have recalled the Inga Arvad incident with some irony when he was handed a report, late in 1961, on one Judith Campbell. It seemed that Judy, as she was known to her friends, had been ringing the White House to speak with the President. Hoover was, of course, well aware of Jack Kennedy's affairs — the prudish bureau chief was obsessed by the need to gather information about the sex-lives of the famous and powerful — and can have had little doubt what the attractive Miss Campbell's connection was with the President's office. The trouble was that the FBI also had information that she was a lover of Sam Giancana, one of the most powerful Mafia bosses in the United States.

Kennedy had met Judy in February 1960, at a party thrown by his close friend Frank Sinatra. She was one of Hollywood's many aspiring actresses and was also known as something of a "party girl"; a facet that endeared her to the hard-playing Sinatra and his circle.

Jack and Judy became lovers and saw each other fairly frequently over the next two years. Judy later claimed that he rang her often and that she had visited him at the White House at least twenty times for intimate lunches. She called him quite often as well. The White House telephone logs recorded seventy calls from Judy Campbell during a fifty-four week period in 1961 and early 1962. Some of those calls were made from a house in Oak Park, Illinois; the home of mobster Sam Giancana.

Whether Giancana was using Judy to get a blackmail angle on Kennedy has never been made clear, but he certainly must have known that he was sharing his girlfriend with the President. Once, when Judy was staying with Giancana in the luxurious Miami Beach Hotel, Kennedy got word to her that he was vacationing alone at Palm Springs and would appreciate a little female company. Apparently with Giancana's blessings she left to join the President immediately.

Scandals

Hoover contacted Bobby Kennedy, Jack's younger brother, then serving as Attorney General. Bobby Kennedy had a particular hatred for organized crime and had personally insisted on the multi-level FBI surveillance on Sam Giancana. First Bobby, then J. Edgar Hoover remonstrated with the President and he was finally persuaded to stop Judy ringing him at the White House. Even so, he continued to see Judy until the summer of 1962.

It may seem insanely foolish of Kennedy to have continued such a dangerous affair once he had been appraised of the facts, but on closer inspection one realizes that it was yet another illustration of his cool political insight. He had no intention of breaking-off an enjoyable relationship and he knew that Giancana could not harm him; in fact, quite the opposite.

One of his former aides later commented on the affair: "Back in those days no reporter in the country would have touched the Judy Campbell story, no one would have believed Jack was screwing around and certainly not with a mobster's woman. If it got out in any way, we would have just said that it's a vicious tale spread by a murderer from Chicago named Giancana because the Kennedy Administration is seriously damaging the mob. We could have easily turned it into a plus for Jack. And Jack knew it."

Various psychological explanations for Jack Kennedy's womanizing have been suggested over the years. Not the most infrequent is the theory that he was trying to live up to his father. Old Joe Kennedy Snr was one of the great American entrepreneurs in every sense of the word. He made a huge fortune from the stock market, from the movie business and, it is alleged, the bootlegging trade during prohibition. Joe Kennedy nursed a life-long chip on his shoulder over his family's exclusion from the East Coast "Brahmin" upper class circles, due to their Irish background. As a result he was as aggressive in his sexual affairs and home life as he was in the business and political worlds, and encouraged his boys to behave in the same way. Jack Kennedy, always a sickly person, is known to have felt inadequate to his father's demands and spent much of his youth fighting with his father's favourite, his older brother Joe Jnr.

During World War II, two events seem to have deeply marked Jack. The first was his own near death when a Japanese destroyer rammed his small "PT" patrol boat (Kennedy was cited for conspicuous bravery in his efforts to get himself and his crew rescued afterwards). The second was the death of Joe Jnr, on a volunteer-only bomber mission against a German V–1 missile base in France. Afterwards Jack Kennedy seems to have been driven by the certainty of his own death and a determination to live life to its fullest before he died. His very poor state of health throughout his life reinforced this drive. He once admitted to a colleague, "The doctors say I've got a sort of slow-motion leukaemia, but they tell me I'll probably last until I'm forty-five."

The American President Calvin Coolidge and his wife were visiting a government farm and were taken on separate tours. As she passed the chicken pen, Mrs Coolidge asked the man in charge how many times a day the rooster mounted the hens. "Dozens of times." "Please tell that to the President" said Mrs Coolidge. When the President visited the pen, the man passed on the message. "And does the rooster choose the same hen each time?" "Oh no – a different one." "Please tell that to Mrs Coolidge."

In this light one can see that Kennedy's hyperactive sex-life was only part of the picture. Everything he did, including his successful run for the presidency, was part of his need to enjoy and excel in life. In his eulogy to his brother, Bobby Kennedy pointed out that at least half of Jack's days had been spent in agony due to his poor health, yet he was one of the most fulfilled people that he had ever known. Jack Kennedy was forty-six-years-old when he was assassinated in Dallas in 1963.

The Profumo Scandal

The recent Palace Pictures film about the Profumo affair was called simply *"Scandal!"* reflecting how much this particular fall from grace seems to represent the whole idea of scandalous behaviour. Many people maintain that it was the publicity surrounding the scandal that lost the Conservatives the election in October 1964. In the general outrage, it was difficult to evaluate who the victims of this scandal actually were.

Britain's population in the early sixties had an abnormally low average age. The post-war baby boomers were attaining their majority, and the staid attitudes of the fifties were slowly giving way to a more casual view of sex and morality. In London, prostitution was booming and night-clubs offered a useful marriage of brothel and bar. The economy was in a healthy state, and people were prepared to spend money on leisure. As Prime Minister Macmillan put it: "Our people have never had it so good." Following the Profumo scandal the satirical magazine *Private Eye* was to alter the quote to "We've never had it so often."

John Dennis Profumo had been the Minister for War in Macmillan's cabinet since July 1960. He had married a popular British actress, Valerie Hobson in 1954. His appearance was grimly respectable: balding, solemn-faced and neatly dressed. It was perhaps his very respectability, his conservative appearance that made his fall from grace so very shocking to the public at large.

For the weekend of 8 July Profumo and his wife were invited by Lord Astor to a party at his country estate, Cliveden, near Maidstone in Kent. More than twenty rich and influential people were to attend. Another party was taking place at Cliveden that weekend, at the cottage of Dr Stephen Ward in the grounds of the estate. He rented the cottage from his friend Astor for the token amount of £1 a year.

Stephen Ward was an osteopath. His charming and refined manner and his habit of name-dropping had gained him a roster of celebrities as both patients and friends. His acquaintance with much of the aristocracy left him perfectly placed to make introductions; he had set up many society marriages. He would allow attractive young women to stay at his flat free of charge, never behaving in a less than gentlemanly fashion with them, simply in order to look at them and to have beautiful escorts when he went out. The spirit of growing sexual freedom in Britain at the time was not limited to the lower reaches of society, and Ward attended and organized expensive parties where group sex was an accepted after-dinner pastime. It was perhaps because his circle of friends encompassed both influential men and poor but attractive women, that he gained a reputation as a procurer.

Among those at Ward's house party this particular weekend was Christine Keeler, a nineteen-year-old night-club hostess whom Ward had taken under his wing. Keeler had left home at sixteen, after a self-induced abortion, and came to London to be a model. She found work as a topless dancer at Murray's Cabaret Club, mingling with the customers between numbers and sometimes accepting money for sex. Ward found her in Murray's and offered her a room in his flat. She became Ward's confidante.

Christine Keeler as a showgirl at Murray's Cabaret Club

Ward had permission from Lord Astor to use the swimming pool in the grounds of the Cliveden estate. On this night Ward had told Keeler that she should swim in the pool naked, as her borrowed costume did not fit her. As she was swimming Lord Astor and John Profumo, who were taking the air in the garden, happened upon the party. Keeler tried to make a grab for her discarded costume, but Ward got to it first and threw it into the bushes. The embarrassed swimmer tried to get out of the pool while covering herself with an inadequately small towel. Lord Astor and Profumo decided to chase her, and it was as the aristocrat and elder statesman were trying to tackle the effectively naked Keeler that the rest of Astor's guests including Mrs Profumo, reached the swimming pool. The two groups of guests mingled and got on well, so much so that the Ward party was invited to meet the other guests at the swimming pool the next night.

This next night Eugene Ivanov, a naval attaché at the Soviet embassy attended the party around the pool. Ward had met him through his illustrious circle of friends and, always keen to develop important acquaintances, he had invited him to the cottage for the weekend. During the evening Profumo tried to get Keeler's phone number from her. The same night Keeler had sex with Ivanov.

This was the beginning of a period during which the British Minister for War and a Soviet naval attaché shared the same lover. Profumo was not particularly careful to conceal his affair, driving with Keeler in his government car, and having sex with her in his own house when his wife was away. He would meet her at Ward's flat in Wimpole Mews, as would Ivanov. However, there is no evidence to suggest that Profumo and Ivanov ever met there, although according to Keeler there were a few near misses. During this period Ward was twice visited by MI5, who advised him to dissociate himself from Ivanov. This, in retrospect was a bad mistake on the intelligence agency's part, as it gave Ward the impression that he had some effect on the exercise of international political power, a delusion that he had secretly fostered anyway. He felt immersed in a world of espionage, and jokingly asked Keeler to learn from Profumo when the Americans intended to site nuclear weapons in Germany. At the time the Soviets were deploying weapons in Cuba, and the information would have been immensely valuable to them.

MI5 soon received information from a defecting Soviet that Ivanov was a spy, and discreetly informed Profumo that he should not have contact with him. The intelligence agency apparently did not know about both men's association with Keeler, despite tentative gossip column items in the press mentioning a certain London flat where a Government car no sooner pulled away, than a Soviet diplomatic vehicle pulled up. Profumo's indiscretion had

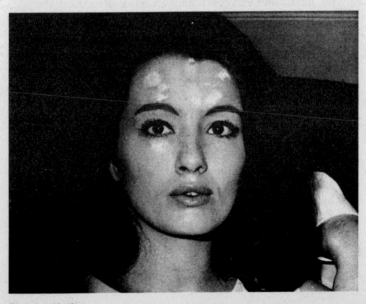

Christine Keeler

also created a wealth of verbal rumours. Impressed by the gravity of the situation, Profumo wrote Keeler a goodbye letter and broke contact with her.

Keeler then went through a succession of boyfriends, moving in and out of Stephen Ward's flat depending on the state of her relationships. She went to America with Mandy Rice-Davies, a friend from her time at Murray's.

All this time Christine Keeler was being harassed by ex-lover "Lucky" Gordon, a West Indian drug dealer and underworld figure. On two occasions "Lucky" held Keeler at knife point for days on end, refusing to let her leave his presence and repeatedly raping her. He had been prosecuted for an assault that involved inserting a knife into a woman's vagina. Gordon would find out where Keeler was living and make nuisance calls or hang around outside waiting for her to leave. For a short time he and Keeler were reconciled and they lived together, but Gordon was obsessively jealous and repeatedly violent.

After Gordon had attacked Keeler she would usually return to Stephen Ward's flat, for comfort and protection. Eventually she became sick of living in fear and bought an illegal handgun and two magazines. In her autobiography "Nothing But . . ." Keeler admits that she had every intention of killing Gordon if he attacked her again.

Keeler became the lover of Johnny Edgecombe, a West Indian associate of "Lucky" Gordon's. After Gordon had again attacked Keeler in public, Edgecombe insisted upon confronting Gordon with the fact that Keeler did not love him, and that she did not want to see him again. When the three of them met in a club, Gordon tried to hit Edgecombe with a chair, and the ensuing fight ended with Edgecombe slashing Gordon's face from forehead to chin. Keeler went into hiding at Stephen Ward's flat, severing all contacts with Gordon and Edgecombe.

Eugene Ivanov was still a close friend of Ward's, visiting him regularly. During the week of the Cuban missile crisis,

Scandals

Ivanov told Ward that his superiors had authorized him to negotiate an unofficial solution with the British Government and asked Ward to use his contacts to get Ivanov meetings with British MPs. Ward had little luck, but managed to get Conservative back-bencher William Shepherd to meet Ivanov at the flat in Wimpole Mews. Nothing came of the meeting but Shepherd became suspicious of the set-up at Ward's flat and conducted his own investigations. He even interviewed Percival Murrays, proprietor of Christine Keeler's old place of work. He then passed his findings on to MI5.

Meanwhile Johnny Edgecombe had tired of waiting for Keeler to come out of hiding. He arrived at Ward's home in a minicab, carrying Keeler's gun. When Mandy Rice-Davies had refused him entry he tried to shoot the lock off the door. When this failed he took a shot at Keeler through a window, missing. The police arrived and Edgecombe was arrested.

Keeler's name in the headlines revived the rumours of the previous year concerning Profumo. George Wigg, the Labour Shadow Spokesman on Defence, who had clashed with Profumo in the commons over the Vassall Spying case received an anonymous phonecall: "Forget about Vassall. You want to look at Profumo."

Keeler took legal advice over her role in the Edgecombe/ Gordon attacks, and realized that if she testified in Edgecombe's trial she would have to admit that she had bought the gun, and that she was the basis for the antagonism between the two men. She also realized the potentially scandalous nature of her joint affairs with Ivanov and Profumo. Ward disassociated himself from her, making a statement to the police suggesting that he was put upon by Keeler, who was always smoking drugs and having sex with West Indians in his flat without his approval. Keeler responded with a statement that portrayed Ward as little better than a perverse, down-market pimp and then sold her story to the *Sunday Pictorial*.

However they did not publish. The facts were known to many people, yet the press were afraid to print them as truth; Profumo's solicitors had cowed them into silence. MI5 knew of the affair by this time also, but they decided that it was best to leave the facts secret, and instructed the police to leave certain avenues of investigation untrodden. Profumo seemed to have escaped once again from the consequences of his ill-considered affair.

A few days before Edgecombe's trial Keeler escaped to Spain. Her absence was a major news story, and the newspapers took the opportunity to insinuate all they dared about Profumo's connections with the missing witness. Finally Labour's George Wigg voiced the question that the newspapers had avoided. During a Parliamentary debate on Press freedom, and thus in a situation immune to threats from Profumo's solicitors, he said: "There is not an Honourable Member in this House . . . who in the last few days has not heard rumour upon rumour involving a member of the Government Front Bench. The Press has got as near as it can — it has shown itself willing to wound, but afraid to strike . . . I rightly use the privilege of the House of Commons to ask the Home Secretary to go to the Dispatch Box — he knows that the rumour to which I refer relates to Miss Christine Keeler and Miss Davies and a shooting by a West Indian — and on the behalf of the Government, categorically deny the truth of these rumours. On the other hand if there is anything in them, I urge the Prime Minister to set up a select committee, so that these things can be dissipated and the honour of the Minister concerned freed from the imputations and innuendoes that are being spread at the present time."

Profumo was not in the House at the time, but when he heard of Wigg's question he prepared a personal statement to be read to the House. Traditionally personal statements to the House are not questioned by other Members, thus it is a matter of honour that they are wholly true. His statement conclusively denied any impropriety in his relationship with Christine Keeler. He admitted meeting both her and Ivanov through Ward, a mutual friend. He threatened libel writs against anyone mentioning the rumours outside the protection of Parliamentary privilege. The Press, that had held back partly out of fear but also because of respect for high office, was enraged by such an obvious lie. Yet they were gagged by Profumo's threats of libel action. They dropped as many damaging hints as they could, but it seemed that Profumo had escaped a possible scandal through sheer nerve and dishonesty.

However, Dr Stephen Ward knew the true facts, and he seemed unwilling to keep them to himself. He was sure that his knowledge would lead to his being framed. He affirmed that Profumo had shared Christine Keeler's favours with Ivanov to both George Wigg and MI5. He wrote to the Home Secretary with the same message. At the same time

Christine Keeler with her friend Paula Hamilton Marshal on their way to court

the CID were receiving anonymous messages suggesting that Ward was a pimp. A substantial power-group wanted Profumo's lie revealed; another group wanted it concealed. Stephen Ward, through his innate urge to be at the hub of important events was setting himself up as a target.

Keeler returned to Britain after being tracked down by the newspapers. Mandy Rice-Davies was arrested for possession of a forged driving license, a charge that a judge later admitted was created merely to prevent her from leaving the country. She spent two weeks in Holloway.

Profumo had gone on holiday to Venice. There, he confessed to his wife that he had lied to the Commons, and that the rumours were true. His letter of resignation and Macmillan's acceptance were published in all newspapers. A vote of no confidence was entered by the Labour Party, and the general feeling was that Macmillan would have to resign. However he succeeded in hanging on, buying time by appointing Lord Denning to investigate the affair.

The police interviewed one hundred and forty people in relation to the allegations about Ward's immoral earnings. Eventually they felt they had enough evidence and Ward was arrested for charges under the Sexual Offences Act. At the Committal Hearing a key police witness, Margaret Richardson lied about Ward's status as her pimp. She admitted at the later trial that it was due to "police pressure". It was clear that there was a great deal of pressure for justice to appear to be done to Ward, Keeler and Rice-Davies. Keeler was sent to prison for nine months for perjury in "Lucky" Gordon's trial. Rice-Davies spent time in Holloway so that she could be a witness against Ward. Ward himself could not bear the feeling of persecution that the police investigations and his trial had brought to him. He overdosed on Nembutal on the night before his trial reached verdict. In his suicide note he wrote: "It's not only fear, it's a wish not to let them get me. I'd rather get myself."

Macmillan finally did resign after some disastrous by-election results in late 1963. Sir Alec Douglas-Hume took over, and was defeated by Harold Wilson in September 1964.

John Profumo was at fault, both for allowing his affair to be noticed and in lying to Parliament about it. He lost his job, but saved his marriage, and his wife remains with him to this day. Christine Keeler had to live with being labelled a tart who could not keep quiet. Although one would imagine her story would guarantee her livelihood, she is by no means wealthy and relies upon social security. Stephen Ward was hounded to death. Keeler recalls that in his heyday Ward attended orgies with the Prosecutors of the "Lady Chatterley's Lover" pornography trial. These friends showed no hurry to help him later on. Eugene Ivanov flew back to the Soviet Union two days after Keeler was first interviewed by the police.

A mystery still remains as to why the police needed one hundred and forty interviews to bring charges of living off immoral earnings. It seems clear that Ward was set up by the authorities as a figure of malign influence in order to explain Profumo's fall. Only his suicide spoilt that manufactured image.

Jeremy Thorpe –
Did the Liberal Leader hire a Hitman?

The trial of Jeremy Thorpe, the leader of the British Liberal Party on a charge of conspiracy to murder, was the single greatest political scandal in the UK since the Profumo affair. The details of the charge were that Thorpe had incited three men – who stood in the dock beside him – to murder the former male model Norman Scott, with whom Thorpe was alleged to have had a homosexual affair.

The publicity surrounding the charge destroyed what

had been an incredibly successful political career. The son of a Conservative MP, Thorpe had been educated at Eton College and Oxford University. At University he had headed many Liberal political groups, finally becoming president of the prestigious Oxford Union Society. He was called to the bar in 1954, and stood for election as Liberal candidate for North Devon in the same year. At the first attempt he lost, but he cut the Tory majority in half. He contested the seat again in 1959, and won by 362 votes. He immediately made a great impression in the House of Commons with his wit and oratory. Only one potential problem existed: in March 1960 a routine security check into Thorpe's background revealed that he had homosexual tendencies. At this time homosexual activity was still a criminal offence. It was also in 1960, on a visit to an Oxfordshire riding stable, that Thorpe met the man who was to precipitate his downfall, Norman Josiffe, later known as Norman Scott.

Josiffe, eleven years Thorpe's junior, was the child of a broken marriage. He had a history of emotional problems and was on probation for larceny. He also claimed that both his parents were dead. Thorpe obviously took a liking to him as he offered him help if ever he needed it. A year later, after an unsuccessful suicide attempt, Josiffe remembered the offer and got in contact with Thorpe. He went to meet him at the House of Commons on 8 November 1961. Afterwards, they went to Thorpe's mother's house in Oxted, Surrey. There, according to Josiffe, their homosexual affair began.

Thorpe allegedly instructed Josiffe to assume the identity of a member of a TV crew in order to allay any suspicions that Thorpe's mother may have had. That night Thorpe went to Josiffe's room with a copy of James Baldwin's homosexual novel *Giovanni's Room*. Later he returned in his dressing gown. According to Josiffe: "He said I looked like a frightened rabbit . . . he just hugged me and called me 'poor bunny' . . . he got into bed with me." Thorpe then sodomized Josiffe. Josiffe denied that he found the experience pleasurable: "I just bit the pillow and tried not to scream." Despite this the affair did continue, Josiffe being given a job on the staff of Len Smith, a Liberal Party official. He accompanied Thorpe on visits to his mother's in Devon and they met in Josiffe's flat near the House of Commons. A problem arose however when Josiffe was accused of stealing the coat of a Mrs Ann Gray. Thorpe basically fixed the trouble for Josiffe, insisting that the police interview take place in his room in the House of Commons, claiming that he was Josiffe's guardian. Shortly afterwards Josiffe moved to work on a farm in Somerset and Thorpe sent him a letter: "take the Ann Gray incident as over and done with". The letter ended: "Bunnies can (and will) go to France."

Josiffe stayed put however, and was soon thrown off the farm when his dog killed some ducks. He tried confessing his "sins" to a Catholic priest, but was denied absolution unless he broke off his relationship with Thorpe. Josiffe was becoming very bitter, and openly discussed a plan to kill Thorpe and then commit suicide. The result was that Josiffe was interviewed by the police. He told them all about his relationship with Thorpe, handing over the "Bunnies can (and will) go to France" letter to confirm his story. The police, not unsurprisingly, did nothing.

Meanwhile, Thorpe had been investigating Josiffe's background, and had discovered that his parents were not dead. This seems to have prompted Thorpe to break off the affair. When Gieves Ltd, a West End outfitter demanded payment for a pair of silk pyjamas that Josiffe had ordered on Thorpe's account, Thorpe told them he would not pay, and that he had no idea of Josiffe's present whereabouts.

In fact Josiffe was in Ireland, once again working with horses. Soon he tried to contact Thorpe again, asking him to lend money for a trip to the Continent. Thorpe provided the money and Josiffe went to Switzerland. However he disliked his job and surroundings and promptly returned without his luggage. With exemplary patience Thorpe offered to try and recover the lost cases. He enlisted the help of fellow Liberal MP Peter Bessel, member for Bodmin. Bessel flew to Dublin to see Josiffe, and found him on the whole likeable. However he told Josiffe that he did not believe the allegations of homosexuality against Thorpe, and demanded proof. Josiffe told him that the luggage in Switzerland contained compromising letters from Thorpe. Bessel agreed to recover them. When the cases finally reached Josiffe, the letters had gone . . .

The cycle of Thorpe casting him off and Josiffe returning when he was broke continued. Undoubtedly some element of blackmail kept Thorpe ready to provide help. In January 1967 Thorpe became head of the Liberal Party. The information Josiffe held now became proportionately more important, and in 1968, according to the prosecution case, Thorpe began to consider killing Josiffe, who had now changed his name to Scott. In a conversation with Bessel over what was to be done with Josiffe/Scott, Thorpe said, "We have got to get rid of him". Bessel asked, "Are you suggesting killing him off?" "Yes," Thorpe replied.

Nothing proceeded immediately. Scott once again threatened Thorpe with revelation, this time of the compromising letters that Bessel had written to him on Thorpe's behalf. He received £2,500 in exchange for the "Bessel File". With the money he moved to a cottage on Exmoor and began to drink heavily and take drugs. Eventually he was contacted by a man who called himself Peter Keene, who told him that his life was in danger, that a hired killer was on his way from Canada to assassinate him. Keene maintained that he had been sent by an "unknown bene-factor" to warn Scott. He asked Scott to come with him in order to meet this unknown figure. Scott refused, but agreed to meet him in the centre of the local town, Combe Martin on 24 October 1975. Scott decided to take his Great Dane along.

"Keene", whose real name was Andrew Newton, met Scott and put him at his ease with his friendly manner. They drove off to the rendezvous. Newton began driving very badly, saying that he was tired. Scott offered to drive. They stopped, and as Scott approached the driver's door he saw that Newton was pointing a Mauser handgun at him. "This is it," said Newton and shot the Great Dane, Rinka, through the head. "It's your turn now," said Newton, but the gun seemed to jam. He jumped into the car and drove away. Scott succeeded in flagging down a car and calling the police.

Newton had not put much effort into concealing his movements, and was arrested soon afterwards. He told the police that Scott had been blackmailing him, and that he had shot his dog in order to scare him. He received two years imprisonment, of which he served slightly more than a year.

Scott did not take this incident as a warning, and in January 1976, when charged with defrauding the DHSS, he did what he had been threatening to do for a long time, he blurted the details of his affair with Thorpe. He told the court that he had been hounded for many years because he had had a homosexual relationship with a Jeremy Thorpe.

Now the story was out, Thorpe immediately denied the allegation. He told Cyril Smith, the Liberal chief whip, that Scott was a blackmailer, extorting money not from him but from Peter Bessel. Thorpe said that Scott knew of an extra-marital affair of Bessel's. Now Thorpe actually had corro-boration for this, Bessel had written him a letter to that effect as a last-ditch line of defence. When Thorpe leaked the letter to ease pressure on himself, Bessel prepared to deny it. Thorpe desperately asked him to wait: "Peter, I'm begging for time."

Inevitably however, the press forced Thorpe to resign.

Jeremy Thorpe leaving the Old Bailey

Scandals

Newton, now freed, sold a sensational story to the *London Evening News*. When Bessel, who was by now disillusioned with Thorpe, commented in print, Thorpe declared war on him, attacking his integrity and honesty. The press meanwhile had found a connection between Newton and Thorpe in the form of three South Wales small businessmen, John Le Mesurier, David Holmes and George Deakin. These men had hired Newton to frighten Scott into leaving Thorpe alone. The Director of Public Prosecutions was less sure, and charged Thorpe, Deakin, Le Mesurier and Holmes with conspiracy to murder.

The case opened at the Old Bailey on 8 May 1979. Soon Peter Bessel was called by the prosecution and seemed to provide damning evidence. He told the court of the 1968 conversation in which Thorpe had first brought up the idea of murder. He also said that he had been the contact between Holmes and Thorpe and described long conversations between the three of them, discussing possible ways of disposing of Scott's body. When Bessel had questioned the morality of killing Scott, Thorpe allegedly replied, "It's no worse than shooting a sick dog."

Bessel also suggested that Thorpe had paid Newton with money embezzled from Liberal Party funds. Taken as a whole the evidence seemed damning. However George Carman QC cross-examined Bessel skilfully, establishing that he had a deal with a newspaper to buy his story. The price would be £50,000 if Thorpe was convicted and only £25,000 if he was not. The suggestion, of course, was that Bessel had a vested interest in seeing Thorpe convicted.

Scott appeared in the witness box, and made a terrible impression on the court. Carman managed to establish that Scott had been boasting about having a homosexual relationship with Thorpe before he went to meet him in the House of Commons for the very first time. This completely undermined Scott's account of his unwillingness on that first night at Thorpe's mother's house.

In his summing-up the judge described Scott as a fraud, a whinger, a whiner and a parasite. On the basis of these remarks, and the generally poor performance of prosecution witnesses, Thorpe and his alleged accomplices were acquitted.

It is difficult to say exactly where the truth lies in the complex web of contradictory evidence surrounding the Thorpe trial. There was strong feeling at the time that the judge's summing-up contained too much conjecture and personal comment about Scott. All that seems clear is that although Scott was torn apart in court and Thorpe was acquitted, it was Thorpe who fell furthest. By the time a verdict was reached, the scandal had destroyed him.

President Richard Milhous Nixon – The Watergate Break-in Scandal

No scandal has shaken the American public as much as the Watergate affair. Indeed, subsequent political scandals have tended to carry the word "gate" as a suffix (i.e. Irangate, Contragate, etc) as if to pay tribute to the grandfather of them all.

At 1 a.m. on the night of 17 June 1972, twenty-four-year-old security guard Frank Mills noticed something odd as he was completing his patrol around the Watergate shopping/office complex in downtown Washington DC. A piece of tape had been placed over the spring catch of a door to the garage basement, preventing it from locking. Unperturbed, he removed the tape and went off to buy a cheeseburger. Forty-five minutes later he returned and found the door had been re-taped. At last realizing that the building was being burgled he rushed to phone the authorities.

Three plain clothes policemen responded to the call and proceeded to search the building. Across the street a lookout in a Howard Johnson motel spotted the armed officers and started to make some desperate telephone calls. He was too late, the officers were already searching the complex's third floor and his accomplices were trapped. Five burglars were found hiding behind desks in the Democratic National Committee offices—the Democrat's election headquarters. All of them were wearing neat suits and blue rubber gloves. They were carrying cameras, rolls of film, equipment suitable for setting-up electronic surveillance (i.e. telephone taps), and around $2,000 in hundred dollar bills. The officers quickly realized that their suspects were hardly run of the mill petty crooks.

At first the burglars gave false names to the police and tried to brazen it out. But, when the police found keys to rooms in the Watergate Hotel on two of them, they rapidly changed their minds and gave their true names. The five burglars were: James McCord, Bernard Barker, Virgilio Gonzalez – a locksmith – Eugenio Martinez and Frank Sturgi. McCord had been an FBI agent and an officer in the CIA. Barker was also a CIA agent. Gonzalez and Martinez were Cuban exiles, and Sturgis was a "soldier of fortune". In court they gave their professions as "anti-communists".

The Democrats were naturally delighted with these events. With a presidential election in the offing, they hoped to discredit Nixon, and if possible prove that he had ordered the bugging of the democratic headquarters. The American public in general was not deeply interested in the scandal; few people seemed to feel that bugging the Democratic headquarters was a particularly serious crime. Understandably, the Democrats, who smelt blood, were determined to alter that opinion – perhaps even to indict the President himself.

The subsequent story of Watergate is a tale of Nixon's attempts to play down the scandal, and of his opponents' determination to play it up and make the utmost political capital out of it. The struggle went on for two years, and culminated in the resignation of Richard Nixon in August 1974. By the time it was all over, most Americans – and in fact, most of the rest of the world – were utterly bored with Watergate, and a full account of all the twists and turns of those two years would probably be equally boring for the reader. In summary, the story is as follows.

Nixon's campaign manager, Attorney General John Mitchell, lost no time in disowning the burglars and insisting that they had acted alone. Nixon quickly confirmed this. But things began to go wrong for Nixon when Press investigators – particularly from the *Washington Post* – learned that $114,000 had been paid into Barker's bank account in Miami two months before the break-in. It was soon established that a large part of this money represented "campaign contributions" for the Campaign for the Re-election of President Nixon, called CRP for short, and known to the press as Creep. It seemed that Creep used some of the money to finance a "dirty tricks" squad known as "The Plumbers" (or White House Special Investigations Unit), and that this included the five burglars. So a link with the Republican party was now established beyond all doubt. The Plumbers also included a former District Attorney, G. Gordon Liddy, and a novelist and CIA agent called Howard Hunt. Orders were passed on to the Plumbers via the President's chief domestic adviser John Ehrlichman.

By August 1972 Nixon was fighting an action in damage limitation; on 29 August he announced that White House counsel John Dean had conducted an investigation that proved that no one on the White House staff knew anything about the burglary. Two weeks later the five "burglars" were charged, and their trial was set for the following January.

The American public was not particularly interested in Watergate, and Nixon was voted back into office by a landslide. Meanwhile, the *Washington Post* was determined to make his second term of office as difficult as possible, and continued to "dig". They struck gold when some anonymous White House informant who called himself "Deep Throat" (and whose identity is still unknown) provided all kinds of inside information about Creep and the Plumbers, and their campaign to discredit the Democrats – if necessary, through "dirty tricks". Nixon's supporters reacted by mounting an attempt to damage the *Post*; its ownership of two Florida TV stations was challenged, and the value of *Post* stock dropped by 50 per cent

The "burglar" trial opened on 8 January, 1973, with two additional defendants, Liddy and Hunt. All seven pleaded – and were found – guilty. Inevitably, the press felt that the guilty plea was simply a method of hushing up the whole affair as soon as possible, and this seemed to be confirmed when the *Post* learned that the defendants had received promises that their families would be taken care of if they went to jail. The sentencing was deferred for two months.

Meanwhile, a Senate Investigation Committee was set up under Democrat Sam J. Ervin. Great embarrassment was caused to Nixon when Patrick Gray, J. Edgar Hoover's successor as head of the FBI, revealed that a great deal of phone tapping had gone on for the four years up to 1972, when the Supreme Court ruled it illegal.

The sentences, when they came, were wildly out of proportion to the offence: twenty years for Liddy, thirty for Hunt, forty each for Barker, Gonzalez, Martinez and Sturgis. McCord was released on bail. He had written a letter to Judge Sirica admitting that there was a cover-up and that higher-ups in the conspiracy had not been named. The Democrats had achieved their aim. By imposing patently outrageous sentences – the equivalent of mediaeval torture – Sirica had cracked the "conspiracy of silence". McCord subsequently told the Senate Committee that both presidential aide John Dean and Jeb Magruder, Deputy Director of Creep, had known about the burglary in advance.

On the same day, 15 April, Nixon summoned Dean to his office and proceeded to ask him a number of leading questions — which led Dean to the correct conclusion that his words were being taped, with a view to being used in the President's defense at some later date.

On 30 April, 1973, Nixon appeared on television to admit that there had been a cover-up — of which he himself had been ignorant — and that Ehrlichman and Bob Haldeman, his chief of staff, had resigned. John Dean also "resigned". So did Richard Kleindienst, John Mitchell's successor as Attorney General. Patrick Gray also resigned as head of the FBI.

The President was obviously involved in a landslide which he could do nothing to prevent; there was nothing he could now do but watch helplessly while the Democrats undermined his administration. In Los Angeles, a man named Daniel Elsberg was on trial for handing to the press secret Pentagon papers about America's involvement in the Vietnam war. He was patently guilty of publishing secrets that could damage his country, but the powerful anti-Vietnam movement chose to regard him as a hero. The case against Elsberg collapsed when the judge, Matthew Byrne, revealed that he had been offered Patrick Gray's job as head of the FBI — obviously as a bribe to make sure of a guilty verdict.

On 13 July, 1973, the last phase of Nixon's downfall began when Alexander Butterfield, a Haldeman aide, revealed the existence of tapes of the President's conversations over the past two years — the implication again being that Nixon had taped conversations to use as evidence in his favour if the necessity arose. Instantly, the chairman of the Committee, Sam Ervin, wrote to Nixon demanding the tapes. Nixon declined, claiming executive privilege. On 22 July, a subpoena was served on him demanding that he produce the tapes.

Ehrlichman and Haldeman were quizzed by the Committee; both pleaded ignorance of the break-in. Now everyone was hitting harder. Nixon offered a summary of the tapes, and when Prosecutor Archibald Cox refused to halt the judicial process, Nixon ordered his dismissal. Attorney General Richardson, who had succeeded Kleindienst, also refused, and resigned; so did his deputy William D. Ruckelshaus. But Nixon got his own way and Cox was finally dismissed.

This undemocratic procedure – which became known as the Saturday Night Massacre – caused such uproar that Nixon was forced to hand over some the tapes – seven of them. One of these proved to contain an eighteen and a half minute gap that could not have been caused accidentally. Nixon finally handed over another fourteen tapes. Then he went on a public relations tour of the country, assuring voters: "I am no crook".

On 1 March, 1974, Haldeman, Ehrlichman and five others were indicted for the Watergate break-in. Nixon was named as an "unindicted conspirator", although this fact was not immediately released.

Now the Committee was demanding a further sixty-four tapes. Nixon released a 1,254 page transcript which he claimed to be complete. Even this contained some damning evidence of Nixon's knowledge of the cover-up. The Committee put out its own transcript of nineteen tapes that revealed that Nixon had been highly selective. Moreover passages described in the Nixon transcript as inaudible or irrelevant turned out to be both audible and relevant. When the Committee demanded two more tapes, Nixon flatly refused.

Finally, the Supreme Court stepped in and ordered him to hand them over. If he refused, he would be impeached – i.e. charged as a criminal. Reluctantly, Nixon handed over a recording that had become known as the "smoking gun tape". It proved beyond all doubt that Nixon had known about the cover-up from the beginning. As the

Committee began its debate on impeachment, Nixon stated: "Whatever mistakes I made . . . the basic fact remains that when the facts were brought to my attention I insisted on a full investigation . . ." It was patently untrue.

Nixon was plainly overwrought — he was reliably reported to be wandering the corridors of the White House at night, making speeches to pictures of dead presidents. The Defense Secretary issued a directive to the armed forces that any orders Nixon gave were to be ignored. He was afraid that, in his desperation, Nixon might attempt a military coup.

On 7 August, 1974, Barry Goldwater, perhaps the staunchest of Nixon's conservative supporters, told Nixon he would vote against him in the impeachment proceedings; so did other senior Republicans. That day, Nixon went on his yacht down the Potomac, and startled his adviser Henry Kissinger by bursting into tears and beating his head against the carpet. The following day Nixon went on television and resigned. But he did so unapologetically, without confessions of guilt. If he is sorry for anything, it was clearly that the burglars had been caught. The following day, as he took his leave of the White House, he raised his fingers in a V for Victory salute.

On 8 September, 1974, the new President, Gerald Ford, issued a pardon for Nixon. A suggestion that all the conspirators should be pardoned was dropped in the face of hostile reaction from Congress.

All the indicted men served short terms in prison. Haldeman served eighteen months, then wrote a best-selling book called *The Ends of Power* in which he admitted that Nixon had been involved in Watergate from the start. John Dean served four months, and his book *Blind Ambition* made him a millionaire. Jeb Magruder served seven months and became a born again Christian. John Mitchell served nineteen months. The terms of the original "burglars" were all commuted to similar short periods. Gordon Liddy served the longest of all — fifty-two months.

Nixon remained unrepentant, and is on record as saying that the whole thing was a storm in a teacup. There is a sense in which he is obviously correct. It was in the interests of the Democrats to represent a mild misdemeanour, worth at most a few months in jail, into a major crime. It has been argued that the real crime was the cover-up, but unless Nixon had simply capitulated to the hysteria at an early stage, it is hard to see what else he could have done. In the last analysis, Watergate reflects little credit on anybody — least of all on the "investigative" journalists who were hailed as the heroes of the affair.

Perhaps the final irony of the whole scandal was that historians are now looking on the Nixon presidency as one of the most successful of the twentieth-century. His ability to adjust foreign policy with the long-term in view led to warmer relations with the Soviet Union. The first Strategic Arms Limitation Treaty (SALT I), arguably the first tangible step towards the end of the cold war, was only made possible by Nixon's efforts. His recognition of communist China and his personal meeting with Chairman Mao Tse-Tung stands as one of the great diplomatic coups in American history. Even his ignominious departure from the White House arguably served an important purpose.

Chapter Six

Royal Embarrassments

R oyals are not immune to the scandals that happen around them – in the past some were even to blame for them. It is very difficult for the royals to maintain a low profile because they are in the public eye the whole time. Queen Caroline decided that as her husband no longer seemed interested in her, she would look elsewhere, without being discreet about it. In the case of Michael Fagin, who was found by the Queen to be sitting on her bed, he had only wanted to chat to her about her security arrangements, or lack of them, when he broke into the Palace.

Queen Caroline – The Only British Queen to be Tried for Adultery

It is something of a mystery why the Prince of Wales, the son of King George III, agreed to marry the fat, ugly and tactless Caroline of Brunswick. It is true that he did it largely to persuade parliament to pay his enormous debts. But he could have married the queen's niece, the beautiful and talented Louise of Mecklenburg-Strelitz. His marriage to Caroline was a disaster for everyone.

George Augustus Frederick, the Prince of Wales, was born in August 1762. Determined that his son would grow up virtuous and serious-minded, George III had him brought up far from the court, according to a strict academic and physical regimen. It had the opposite effect: the prince became a rebel, a spendthrift and a waster. At the age of seventeen he embarked on an affair with an actress, Mary Robinson, and his letters to her had to be bought back eventually for £5,000. The prince became a member of a hard-drinking, hard-gambling set, which included the Whig politician Charles James Fox – one of his father's chief enemies – and the playwright Sheridan. He began to run up vast debts. He voted for Fox – and against his father – when Fox's India Bill came before parliament but the Whig politician lost and was dismissed. When he was twenty-three, the prince fell in love with the beautiful Catholic, Mrs Fitzherbert, and although she fled to France to escape his attentions, he finally persuaded her to go through a secret marriage. But constancy was not one of his strong points and he soon took another mistress, Lady Jersey.

By the time he was thirty, the prince was an embarrassment to his father and intensely unpopular with the British public. His debts now amounted to £630,000 – many millions in present-day terms – and Pitt's administration showed no eagerness to find the money. So when it was suggested by his father that he should marry and furnish an heir, he agreed on condition that parliament paid his debts.

Caroline of Brunswick was short, plump and ugly, and she suffered from body odour – probably as a result of infrequent washing. Lady Jersey, the prince's current mistress, may have pushed him into marrying Caroline rather than the beautiful Louise of Mecklenburg-Strelitz as she would be less of a rival. On 5 April 1795, at St James's Palace, the prince was introduced to Caroline; he was shattered. He staggered to the far end of the room and called for a brandy. He went on drinking brandy for three days until the marriage ceremony. On the honeymoon – with Lady Jersey also in attendance – he seems to have done his duty as a husband, for Caroline discovered she was pregnant soon thereafter. But the prince found her unbearable and stayed as far away from her as possible; in the following year he wrote her a letter saying that, "our inclinations are not in our power", but that being polite to one another was. When she received the letter, Queen Caroline was with the politician George Canning and asked him what he thought it meant; Canning replied that it seemed to give her permission to do as she liked. Whereupon Queen Caroline proceeded to do just that with Canning.

What no one realized at the time was that the royal line of Hanover suffered from the disease known as porphyria, the "royal disease", a genetic disorder in which, due to an enzyme defect, the body accumulates large quantities of porphyrins (precursors of red blood pigment). The disease affects the digestive tract, the nervous system, the circulatory system and the skin; it causes psychotic disorders and epilepsy. George III had several attacks of it and died insane. The Prince of Wales was also subject to it and so was Caroline — two of her brothers were imbeciles, probably due to porphyria. It may explain Caroline's utter lack of self-control and her tendency to behave outrageously which led many to suspect she was insane.

Rejected by her husband she retired to a house in Blackheath and behaved in a manner that led Lady Hester Stanhope to call her "a downright whore". She had a Chinese clockwork figure in her room which, when wound up, performed gross sexual movements; she was also given to dancing around in a manner that exposed a great deal of her person.

In 1806, rumours that a four-year-old child in her entourage, William Austin, was her illegitimate son, led to what became known as "the Delicate Investigation". A Royal Commission repudiated the charge and found Lady Douglas, who had started the rumour, guilty of perjury. But years later, Caroline told her lawyer's brother that the child was the natural son of Prince Louis Ferdinand of Prussia, who had always been her love. Mrs Fitzherbert was to state later that Caroline had secretly married Prince Louis before she married the Prince of Wales.

Scandals

Finally, in August 1814, Caroline decided to leave England. In Geneva, at a ball given in her honour, she shocked her hosts by dancing naked to the waist. In Naples she became the mistress of King Joachim, Napoleon's brother-in-law. When she left Naples — at the time Napoleon escaped from Elba — she had with her Napoleon's courier, a coarsely handsome Italian named Bartolomeo Bergami, a former quartermaster in a regiment of hussars. This swarthy, bearded, intensely masculine character looked like a brigand from a Drury Lane play. He travelled with her to Munich, Tunis, Athens, Constantinople and Jerusalem, and when they settled in her villa near Pesaro they behaved as man and wife.

James Brougham, her lawyer's brother, now wrote to England suggesting that the prince — he was now Prince Regent (his father having become insane) — should obtain a legal separation from Caroline so she could never become queen of England. But the prince wanted divorce or nothing. So nothing came of this suggestion.

George III finally died in January 1820 and his son became George IV. Caroline of Brunswick was now Queen Caroline. The government quickly offered her £50,000 a year if she would agree not to return to England. In a fury, Caroline hurried across the Channel. Her husband was one of the most unpopular men in the country and on that count many people espoused her cause. To the intense embarrassment of the government, she settled at Brandenburg House, in Hammersmith. And on 17 August the government took the offensive by hauling her in front of the House of Lords. Its aim was to dissolve the marriage on the grounds that Caroline had engaged in "a most unbecoming and degrading intimacy" with Bergami, "a foreigner of low station". But the government had bitten off more than it could chew. Noisy mobs demonstrated in favour of Caroline and the House of Lords had to be surrounded by two strong timber fences. The queen's coach was always surrounded by a cheering crowd. After fifty-two days the divorce clause was carried. But the oratory of Henry Brougham caused a turn in the tide and when the Bill was given its final reading, it had only a pathetic majority of nine. The Lords decided to drop it.

The coronation was scheduled for 29 April 1821. The queen wrote to the Prime Minister, Lord Liverpool, to ask what kind of a dress she ought to wear for the coronation. He replied that she could "form no part of that ceremony". But when George was crowned, Caroline arrived at the Abbey dressed in a muslin slip and demanded to be admitted. When she shouted, "The queen — open!", pages opened the doors. She continued with "I am the queen of England." An official roared, "Do your duty, shut the Hall door", and the door was slammed in her face. Undaunted, Caroline drove back to Brandenburg House and sent a note to the king asking for a coronation "next Monday".

She died two weeks later, on 7 August 1821 — so suddenly that it was widely rumoured that she had been poisoned. When her body was on its way to the ship that would take it back to Brunswick, there were riots at Kensington Church, bricks were thrown, and two men were shot by the Life Guards. Caroline was buried in Brunswick Cathedral, with an inscription on her coffin: The Injured Queen Of England.

George IV remained intensely unpopular. He lived on for only nine years after the death of Caroline. The major issue of the time was Roman Catholic emancipation (England had been anti-Catholic since the time of Elizabeth I, and George I had come to the throne of England from Hanover because of the Act that prevented a Catholic from becoming king of England.) As Prince of Wales, George had been in favour of Wellington who, as prime minister, carried the act of parliament that finally achieved Catholic emancipation (although Wellington was himself basically opposed to it, believing it would finally destroy English rule in Ireland — as it did.) George IV became hysterical about the issue and threatened to use the royal veto. But the throne no longer held the political power it had under George III, and he was reluctantly forced to accept Catholic emancipation. After that, the king's health deteriorated swiftly and he died on 26 June 1830. He had a portrait of Mrs Fitzherbert round his neck on his death bed. But the two had been estranged for many years — ever since, at a dinner in honour of Louis XVIII in 1803, he had made sure there was no fixed place for her at table, so she must sit "according to her rank". After that insult, she had retired from the court.

The Baccarat Scandal — The Tranby Croft Case

His Highness Albert Edward, Prince of Wales — the son of Queen Victoria — seems to have been in many ways a rather unsavoury character. He was an incorrigible seducer of women, who spent most of his time drinking, playing cards, and indulging in slightly sadistic forms of horseplay. At least one of his friends — Christopher Sykes — ruined himself trying to keep up with the Prince's extravagant way of life. Another, Sir William Gordon Cumming, Bart., a Scottish landowner, also owed his ruin — although in a slightly less direct manner — to his spoiled and unreliable friend.

Gordon Cumming seems to have been rather a disagreeable character, noted for his rudeness and boorishness; the *Sporting Times* described him as "possibly the handsomest man in London, and certainly the rudest". On meeting a medical acquaintance in the courtyard of Buckingham Palace he is said to have enquired: "Hello, is one of the servants sick?"

On 8 September 1890, the Prince of Wales was a guest at Tranby Croft, the house of Arthur Wilson, a rich Hull shipowner. By his special request, Gordon Cumming had also been invited to Tranby Croft. Cumming was at the time a lieutenant-colonel in the Scots Guards.

After a late dinner, the guests listened to some music, then settled down to play baccarat – a card game which has something in common with both roulette and bingo. A dealer hands out a card, face downwards, to two sets of players who sit on either side of him. The aim is to get eight or nine. The dealer looks at his own two cards, and he may "declare". Or he may offer another card to the two lots of players. When either a player or the dealer has eight or nine, he has won. It is a game of chance. The players may stake what they like on the game, and the dealer, like the croupier in roulette, either wins or loses.

The players must sit with their money – or counters representing money – in front of them. The cheating of which Gordon Cumming was accused, consisted in quietly adding a few counters to his stake after the cards had been declared in his favour. It was the son of the house, Arthur Stanley Wilson, who thought he saw Gordon Cumming doing this. He quietly drew the attention of another guest, Berkeley Levett, to this. Levett watched carefully and was soon convinced that he had also seen Gordon Cumming add to his stake after he had won, so increasing his winnings. Later that evening, when the game was finished, he told his mother, and his brother-in-law, Lycett Green, what he had seen. It was decided that the best thing to do was to watch Gordon Cumming carefully the next evening to see if he cheated again.

They did this on the evening of 9 September and five of them – Lycett Green and his wife, and the two Wilson parents and their son – were all convinced they saw Gordon Cumming cheating.

Now this was a serious business – not because of the money involved – for Gordon Cumming had only won £228 in two nights' play, but because he was there at the invitation of the Prince of Wales. Albert Edward — later Edward VII — already had a bad reputation as a gambler and ladies' man, and was often pilloried in the Press. The first thought of his hosts — and they seem to have been social climbers — was to save the Prince from scandal.

Other guests were let into the secret, including Lord Coventry and his assistant General Owen Williams, a close friend of Gordon Cumming. The Prince was told by Coventry that Gordon Cumming had been seen cheating at baccarat, then Coventry and General Williams went to Gordon Cumming, who was in the smoking room, and told him that he had been accused by Lycett Green and young Wilson of cheating at baccarat. Gordon Cumming was indignant and said, "Do you believe the statements of a parcel of inexperienced boys?" After dinner, Coventry, Williams and the Prince of Wales all confronted Gordon Cumming, who continued to insist on his innocence. And later, a document was presented to Gordon Cumming, which he was asked to sign. It declared that, in exchange for the silence of the witnesses against him, Gordon Cumming would solemnly undertake never again to play cards. If he did not sign it, he was told, he would have to leave the house immediately and be proclaimed a cheat on every racecourse in England. Gordon Cumming decided to sign.

The mad Roman emperor Caligula made his horse, Incitatus, a consul. The animal would dine with the emperor at banquets. Even after Caligula was assassinated, and his uncle Claudius became emperor, the horse retained its position.

Far from "hushing up" the scandal, all this secrecy only made it a better subject for gossip. By the next day it was being openly discussed on Doncaster Racecourse. And three months later, on 27 December 1890, Gordon Cumming received an anonymous letter from Paris saying that the scandal was being discussed in Paris and Monte Carlo. Belatedly, he decided to sue. He was demanding an apology from the Wilsons, the Lycett Greens, and Berkeley Levett. Understandably, they refused. Gordon Cumming's solicitors issued a writ for slander.

Sir Edward Clarke was briefed for the prosecution and Sir Charles Russell for the defence – Russell had a reputation of being quite as rude and arrogant as Gordon Cumming. The judge was the Lord Chief Justice himself, the Right Honourable John Duke Bevan Coleridge, a close friend of Russell.

The case opened on 1 June 1891. The defence was one of justification – that Gordon Cumming had not been slandered because he really had cheated. There were no spectacular revelations and no dramatic surprises. The Prince of Wales appeared in the witness box but his evidence was neither for nor against Gordon Cumming. The prosecution failed to shake the witnesses who thought they had seen Gordon Cumming cheat, although he scored a few good points. Gordon Cumming explained that he signed the paper "because it was the only way to avoid a terrible scandal". Clarke's final speech was so brilliant that it looked for a while as if Gordon Cumming had won after all. But the judge's summing up was against Gordon Cumming, his central point being that surely an innocent man would not have signed a paper virtually admitting his guilt. One writer on the case has described the summing up as "polished, skilful and fiendishly unfair". The jury took only thirteen minutes to find the defendants not guilty. They were awarded their costs. Gordon Cumming – now a socially ruined man – slipped out of court immediately after the verdict. The crowd hissed the jurors, and even tried to attack the defendants as they left the court; this was probably due less to a conviction that Gordon Cumming was innocent than to an intense dislike of the Prince of Wales.

The following day, Gordon Cumming married his 21-year-old fiancée, an American heiress named Florence Garner, who had stuck to him throughout his ordeal. She remained convinced to the end of her life that her husband had been deliberately "framed" by the Prince of Wales because of a disagreement about a lady. It is true that "Bertie" (as the Prince was known) was a petty and vindictive man — he continued to persecute Gordon Cumming for the rest of his life — but there seems to be no evidence for Lady Gordon Cumming's assertion. The Gordon Cummings spent most of their lives on their Scottish estate and seem to have been reasonably happy together.

The Buckingham Palace Security Scandal

House break-ins have become so common in London that it has become a genuine oddity to see one reported in the media. Yet in the summer of 1982 one particular break-in caused such a furore that questions were asked in the House of Commons and calls were made for the resignations of both the Chief of the Metropolitan Police and the Home Secretary. Oddly enough, the cause of so much fuss was not a burglar or a spy, but an unemployed labourer trying to do Queen Elizabeth a favour.

Thirty-two-year-old Michael Fagan broke into Buckingham Palace *twice* in the months of June and July 1982 and might have gone undetected both times if he had not felt it was his duty to tell Her Majesty that her palace security was shockingly poor.

Michael Fagan, the Buckingham Palace intruder – the Queen awoke to find him sitting on the end of her bed

Fagan later claimed that he had noticed that Buckingham Palace's security was "a bit lax" during a sightseeing trip with his two young children. He became increasingly disturbed by this risk to the Royal family – for whom he had great admiration – and eventually decided to break into the palace as an act of public-spiritedness. "I wanted to prove the Queen was not too safe," he said later.

Fagan must also have been inspired by the fact that a year before, in the summer of 1981, three West Germans had been found peacefully camping in the palace grounds. When questioned by police they said that they had arrived in London late at night and had climbed over the palace railings in the belief they were entering a public park. They had camped there totally undisturbed until the next morning. A rueful palace spokesman later admitted that this was not the first time that this sort of thing had happened.

On the night of 7 June 1982, Fagan clambered over the iron railings that surround the palace and wandered into Ambassadors Court. Here he found a sturdy drain pipe and proceeded to shin his way up to the roof. On the way he paused to look in at a lighted window. The occupant, housemaid Sarah Jane Carter, was reading in bed and happened to look up when Fagan was looking in. He moved on quickly and the housemaid, shaken and partially convinced that she had been seeing things, called security. They decided not to investigate.

After climbing fifty feet – no small feat in the dark – Fagan reached a flat roof that adjoined the royal apartments. He opened a window and climbed in. Over the next half hour he wandered about quite freely, crossing several infra-red security beams as he did so. These had been fitted incorrectly, like the window alarm, and failed to go off.

During his walk-about he paused to admire the various royal portraits and had a brief rest on the throne. He also came across some royal bedrooms – those of Mark Phillips and the Duke of Edinburgh – the first he decided not to bother and the second turned out to be elsewhere. He then entered the Post Room and found a fridge containing a bottle of Californian white wine. Expecting to be arrested at any moment he decided to relax a bit first. He had drunk half the bottle by the time he realized that nobody was coming to get him, so he put it down and left by the risky way he had entered.

Just over a month later, on the night of 9 July, he drank a fair amount of whisky and set out to repeat his performance. Once again he entered the palace with no difficulties. This time though, he was clearly suffering from stress and too much booze. He smashed a royal ash-tray with the intent of cutting his wrists with the jagged edge, but in doing so cut his hand. Thus, looking for a suitable place to kill himself and dripping blood on the carpet, he came across a door that pronounced itself to be the entry to the Queen's bedroom.

Her Majesty awoke to find Michael Fagan sitting on the edge of her bed, nursing his wounded hand and mumbling in a quiet voice. Speaking reassuringly to him she quietly reached for the alarm button by her bed, but unfortunately it had been incorrectly wired and failed to work. When she realized that nobody was coming, she marshalled considerable courage and picked up the bedside telephone — this apparently didn't bother Fagan in the least. The telephone connected her directly to the palace switchboard and she asked them to put her through to security. Unfortunately the police guard had already knocked-off for the night and nobody else in the vicinity could be raised. Her footman was out in the grounds walking the royal corgis and the nightmaid was working in a room out of earshot of a telephone. The Queen kept a brave face in what must have been a nightmare situation and kept on chatting with the intruder.

Eventually Fagan asked for a cigarette and the Queen, pointing out she was a non-smoker, said she would go and get one from a member of staff. By this time the footman, Paul Whybrew, had returned from walking the dogs and quickly went in to confront the intruder. Fagan quietly insisted that all he wanted to do was talk with *his* Queen. Whybrew said that was fine, but in all fairness he should let her get dressed first. Fagan agreed and went with the footman and a maid to a nearby pantry. He waited there quietly until the police eventually arrived and arrested him.

Despite the fact that Michael Fagan gave a full and detailed confession of both break-ins, the police and crown prosecution faced a difficult problem. It is a peculiarity of

Scandals

English law that entering another person's property is not a criminal offence unless it can be proved that it was done with an intent to commit a crime (Fagan could have been charged with trespassing, but that would have merely been a civil offence). Thus, rather ridiculously, Fagan was tried in the Old Bailey for the theft of half a bottle of wine (valued by the court at £3) that was technically owned by the Prince and Princess of Wales.

The trial contained some farcical scenes. When Mrs Barbra Mills, acting for the prosecution asked Fagan: "It wasn't your drink was it?" He replied: "It wasn't my palace either." "It was not your right to drink it," she insisted, to which Fagan countered: "Well, I'd done a hard day's work for the Queen, showing her how to break her security." He went on to point out that Her Majesty was lucky that somebody as public-spirited as himself had broken into her apartments; "I mean, I could have been a rapist or something!"

The jury acquitted Fagan of the crime of theft, but he was held in custody on an unconnected charge of taking and driving away a car without the owners permission, to which

Queen Elizabeth I, known as the Virgin Queen, is in fact believed to have had several lovers. One of the oddest was Francis, Duke of Alencon. The Duke, once described as a 'hideous dwarf', had suffered from smallpox which had stunted his growth and scarred his body. As a result of the disease, his nose had divided down the middle and pointed in two distinct directions. This, his enemies said, was symbolic of his two-facedness. Francis' weird physique and bumpy skin led Elizabeth to nickname him her petit grenouille, or little frog.

he had also admitted. His second trial took place that October and after he had pleaded guilty, the judge ordered him to be placed in the care of a high security mental hospital. Despite the fact that it was pressed by several-doctors that he should be held without time limit, he was given the right to appeal.

In January of the following year the psychiatric review board found that he was "not fully recovered", but on the grounds that he offered no threat to the community allowed his release. Perhaps predictably, angry questions were asked in the House of Commons.

The mortified police officers in charge of palace security might have hoped for a bit of peace and quiet in which to put their house in order, but this was not to be. Fagan's break-in indirectly sparked-off another, if unconnected, scandal involving one of their most senior officers.

Commander Michael Trestrail, MVO, was the Queen's personal bodyguard and a man of impeccable reputation. He had served in the Royal Protection Group for sixteen years and had been awarded membership of the Royal Victorian Order. Four months before the arrest of Fagan, he had successfully passed the infamous "positive vetting" process; a rigorous investigation of all aspects of an individual's life, designed to weed-out security risks. Yet it took only one telephone call to wreck his career.

Trestrail was a closet homosexual and had indulged in frequent liaisons with male prostitutes over the years. On reading the press reports of the Fagan break-in an ex-lover of Trestrail's, male prostitute Michael Rauch, decided to try to sell his story to the Fleet Street papers. The newspaper he contacted turned him down and decided to report the matter to the Palace. Rauch was taken in by Scotland Yard for questioning and Trestrail resigned immediately. During his interrogation, Rauch admitted to the police that he had tried to blackmail Trestrail some time before; an event that had, not surprisingly, marked the end of their relationship.

Scandals

This disclosure worked an increasingly ugly media mob into a frenzy.

By indulging in a promiscuous, homosexual secret life, Trestrail, it was argued, had left himself open to blackmail by *anybody*, including those who might wish to assassinate the Queen. This belief was refuted by a subsequent official enquiry into the affair. It was found that Trestrail had known he was homosexual since his teens, and though generally attempting to suppress this aspect of himself, he often found it impossible to do so; especially when drunk. Even so, the Commission reported that he had carried out his duties in an exemplary fashion and his private practices had not breached palace security in any way; in fact, only Rauch and another male lover had known of his position at the palace.

Even so, the damage was done. The media trial, which had concentrated on the Commander's homosexuality rather than on his promiscuity, had ruined any chance of his being reinstated. Trestrail took early retirement on a reduced pension.

Later that month, as if to bring everyone back down to earth, the Irish Republican Army (IRA) provided a genuine example of breached security. On 20 July, a car bomb exploded in Hyde Park, killing three members of the Household Cavalry as they rode from their barracks to the changing of the guard ceremony at Whitehall. Twenty-three people were injured and a number of horses were killed or injured so badly they had to be put down. Two hours later, a second bomb went off under a bandstand in Regent's Park during a lunchtime concert by the band of the Royal Greenjackets. Six bandsmen were killed in the blast and twenty-eight people were injured. The Queen, although visibly shaken by the events of the last month, continued with all of her official engagements, although under rigorously tightened security.

Queen Victoria – The haemophiliac gene

Queen Victoria, the British queen whose name is synonymous with staid sexual attitudes and exaggerated propriety, may have been illegitimate. The theory is put forward in the book *Queen Victoria's Gene* by D. M. Potts and W. T. W. Potts

Their theory rests upon the fact that some of Queen Victoria's offspring carried the gene for haemophilia, an inherited disease that prevents the blood from clotting. The disorder only effects male offspring; female children with the gene pass it on to their children without being affected.

It is known from the meticulous records of European royal houses that Edward, Duke of Kent, Victoria's supposed father, was not a sufferer. Records relating to Princess Victoire, Victoria's, mother do not exist. However, by the time that she married the Duke of Kent, Victoire had already married once, and produced two children. If she were a carrier, one would expect haemophilia to show up in these two children, or in their descendants. Records show that that branch of the royal family tree was free from the disease. It is therefore very unlikely that Victoire had inherited the disease.

So where did the gene come from? It could have been a fresh mutation in Victoria or her mother. In other words, the disease could have started spontaneously in either of the two women. As only 1 in 100,000 people per generation develop the haemophilia mutation, this is unlikely. This leaves the possibility that the Duke of Kent was not Victoria's father.

The authors of *Queen Victoria's Gene* suggest that Victoire could have chosen a lover to father her child because her husband Edward was infertile. Evidence for this, they say, can be found in the fact that Edward's mistress, with whom he slept for many years, never got pregnant. This was very uncommon in the early nineteenth century. William IV's mistress, for example, had ten children over the course of their affair.

But why would Victoire cuckold her husband? At the time of Victoria's birth no child of George III had managed to have a legitimate, living child. George IV himself had no heirs. His brother William, who succeeded him, was beginning to look to old too produce a successor. And so it proved.

It seems possible that the phrase 'Victorian values' may have to be redefined.

Queen Victoria and John Brown

Scandal involving the widowed Queen Victoria and her Court favourite, ghillie John Brown, reached such proportions in the 1860s that there were genuine fears for the future of the monarchy in Britain.

Disenchantment with the monarchy stemmed from the Queen's virtual disappearance from public life, following the death of the Prince Consort in 1861. Now rumours of her 'affair' with John Brown, the one-time stable lad who had been appointed Victoria's Personal Highland Servant — with explicit instructions to take orders from no one but herself — fell on doubly fertile ground, both within the Establishment and with the mob.

That Queen Victoria and John Brown loved each other is a matter of record. After Brown's death in 1883, she wrote to his brother Hugh: 'So often I told him that no one loved him more than I did or had a better friend than me . . . and he answered, "Nor you than me. No one loves you more." ' What has always remained the subject for speculation, and scandal, is if that love was strictly platonic.

In his book *Queen Victoria's Private Life*, author E. E. P. Tisdall (who discounted the notion that the affair was platonic) says that a pamphlet entitled *Mrs John Brown* was privately printed in Britain '. . . to circulate very widely in stately homes and servant halls . . . The pamphlet declared that the Queen had married John Brown at a secret ceremony. It was never discovered who had paid for the printing and organized the distribution of the pamphlet, but a suggestion was made that the money came from the funds of the Republican party, which was active and growing, as might be expected with such a queer state of affairs existing around the throne . . .'

By July 1867, government fears of a hostile demonstration against the Queen were such, that an excuse was invented to cancel a military review in Hyde Park rather than risk her attendance there in the company of John Brown. Although she had agreed, reluctantly, to the Prime Minister's suggestion to leave Brown at home to avoid possible incidents 'of an unpleasant nature', the Cabinet feared she might defy ministerial advice and take Brown anyway. So, the assassination in far-off Mexico of the Emperor Maximilian (a distant relative, by marriage, of

---

Stella Newborough (1773–1843) was a strange woman. Born to a peasant family in Modigliana, Tuscany, she married twice, first to an English Lord and then to a Russian baron, thereby obtaining a position on the periphery of Europe's aristocracy. But Stella had further ambitions: she claimed that her father had swapped her on birth with Louis-Philippe of Orleans, who was soon to be King of France. Not surprisingly, he was somewhat reluctant to give up this esteemed position – especially as she had no proof whatsoever – and Stella's hopes were never realized. Nonetheless, she continued her campaign until her very deathbed, calling Louis-Philippe 'the involuntary usurper of rights which henceforth he cannot keep without guilt'.

---

the Queen), was used as a pretext to put the Court back into mourning and cancel the review altogether.

The year 1871 saw the Republican movement reach its zenith in Britain and not only because of her supposed dalliance with Brown. In an age when 15s a week was a factory hand's wage, a request that Parliament should approve a dowry of £30,000, plus an annuity, on the Queen's daughter, Princess Louise's marriage to the Marquis of Lorne, dismayed even the most ardent royalist supporters. The Queen herself was even accused in a pamphlet of misappropriating public funds. Signed by a critic styling himself 'Solomon Temple', and headed 'What Does She Do With It?', the pamphlet complained that cash saved from Civil List funds was diverted to her own account.

Neglect of royal duties was still the main weapon in the Republican armoury, however. *The Times* labelled Queen Victoria 'The Great Absentee', while to the *Pall Mall Gazette* she had become 'The Invisible Monarch'. When she fell ill in the autumn of that year no medical bulletins were issued, so that the country remained unaware of her condition even though, at one stage, she was apparently not expected to live another twenty-four hours. In contrast, when the Prince of Wales (himself no stranger to scandal) went down that winter with typhoid fever – the same illness which had killed his father ten years earlier – the whole nation prayed for his recovery. This time, bulletins were issued as the Prince's condition reached crisis point, so the public attitude to the Royal Family changed to one of compassion and sympathy. ('An epidemic . . . of typhoid loyalty', sneered the anti-royalist *Reynold's News*.) So complete was the turn-around, however, that by mid-December 1871, when the royal recovery was assured, republicanism in Britain was a spent force.

Now it was Brown's turn to benefit from the wind of change. On 27 February 1872 a Thanksgiving Service for the Prince's recovery was held at St Paul's Cathedral. Two days later the Queen drove through Regent's Park in an open carriage, accompanied by her sons Alfred and Leopold, to thank her subjects for their demonstration of loyalty. Brown was on the box, as always. As the carriage re-entered Buckingham Palace a young man scaled the railings, ran up and pointed a pistol at the Queen's face. In the split-second of confusion which followed the two Princes hesitated, as did the mounted equerries nearby. Brown alone proved equal to the occasion. As the Queen screamed, 'Save me!' and flung herself against her Lady-in-Waiting, Lady Jane Churchill, he leapt down and shouldered the gunman aside, then pursued him as he made for the other side of the carriage. He described what happened next to Bow Street magistrates, 'I took hold o' him wi' one o' my hauns, and I grippit him wi' the other by the scruff o' the neck . . . till half a dizzen had a grip o' him, grooms, equerries, I kenna' how mony there was . . .'

The pistol was later found to be defective, the intruder mentally unstable, but none of that detracted from John Brown's courage or presence of mind. In the eyes of the public, at least, he was transformed at a stroke from villain to hero. The Queen presented him with a new award, the Devoted Service Medal, which carried with it an annuity of £25 (but lapsed with his death; John Brown was the sole recipient). She later made him 'John Brown, Esquire' and he was listed in *Whitaker's Almanack* as a member of the household, at a salary of £400 a year.

After his death (from erysipelas) in 1883, aged only fifty-six, he lay in state for six days, in the Clarence Tower at Windsor. His Court Circular obituary occupied twenty-five lines, compared with Disraeli's five lines, two years earlier. The Queen attended his funeral service at Windsor, although most of her family found excuses to be elsewhere. Her card on his coffin read: 'A tribute of loving, grateful, and ever-lasting friendship and affection from his truest, best, and most faithful friend, Victoria. R & I.' Five hundred mourners attended his burial at Craithie, on 5 April 1883. His opponents within the Establishment were to have the last word, however. Encouraged by the success of her previous book, *More Leaves from the Journal of a Life in the Highlands*, which she had dedicated to Brown, the Queen now declared her intention of writing *The Life of Brown*. Her household was appalled, knowing it could only revive the scandal, but lacked the courage to say so. It was left to the Dean of Windsor (The Reverend Randall Davidson, later Archbishop of Canterbury) to urge her, after reading the rough draft, not to publish. When she persisted, he offered to resign – and the Queen gave in.

After his mother's death in 1901, Edward VII inflicted the final indignities on Brown's memory, by ordering her photographs of him to be burned, and his quarters at Windsor turned into a games room. Author Tom Cullen wrote a fitting epitaph for the best-loved and most hated of all British royal servants in his book *The Empress Brown*: 'Although John Brown has been dead for eighty-six years, his bones still rattle in the Royal closet at Windsor, where, as a subject for scandal he is regarded as second to the Abdication . . .'

Chapter Seven

They Lost a Fortune

T hinking yourself above others will eventually bring about
your downfall. Ignoring the law and dictating to those
around you will, at the end of the day, only serve to alienate those
people.

Leona and Harry Helmsley

Leona Helmsley, the Queen of Mean who owned a fortune in
New York hotels, once told her housekeeper: "We don't pay
taxes. Only the little people pay taxes." Three years later this
statement was to help land the woman everyone loved to
hate in jail for tax evasion. The hotel magnate apparently
forgot that she was not exempt from paying $1.7 million in
taxes just because she considered herself royalty.

"We did it for the little people," said one juror after her
conviction in a New York courtroom in 1989. According to
investigators, who were helped by over 100 former
Helmsley employees, the couple had disguised $4 million
of personal spending as business expenditure. After she was
convicted of five counts of tax evasion, filing false returns
and conspiring to defraud the taxman, the New York City
tabloids went crazy with headlines like "For hotel queen, a
pen-house, maybe?", and "Rhymes with Rich . . ." with a
picture of Helmsley next to it.

The story first broke after a disgruntled employee told
the New York Post in 1985, that the Helmsleys were
claiming improvements to their $8 million twenty-eight-
room Jacobean-style Connecticut mansion as business

expenditures, so they could deduct it from their taxes. After a year of investigation, the paper splashed the headline: "Helmsley Scam Bared", and threw some cold water on the couple's good fortunes. The paper reported that millions of dollars in renovation bills were falsified as business expenses and charged to Manhattan office buildings.

Her lawyer used the defence that she was "a tough bitch" who incurred such fear among her staff that they independently resorted to faking invoices to minimize the time they had to spend in her company.

Despite legal appeals and tearful pleas to the judge to stay out of jail due to ailing health ("Jail would be a death sentence," she said), Helmsley was sent to prison in April 1992 at the age of seventy-one and became inmate number 15113–054. She will trade a life of luxury for a shared cell at the Federal Medical Centre in Lexington, Kentucky where she will not find room service – inmates are expected to clean their rooms and make their own beds as well as join the prison workforce of laundry, sewing or grounds-keeping duty. Helmsley left her Park Lane Hotel in Manhattan by limousine and flew to what will be her new home for the next four years, in her personal Boeing 727. Her eighty-three-year-old husband, Harry, worth $5 billion, escaped prosecution because he was ruled mentally incompetent to stand trial.

Barbara Hutton's life changed on her twenty-first birthday in 1930. She inherited $20 million ($148 million today) from her grandfather, Frank Woolworth, a tycoon who owned the five and dime chain-store which bears his name. Hutton spent most of her fortune on her husbands – all seven of them, including the actor Cary Grant.

The woman who launched an advertising campaign which featured her as the "Queen" standing guard at the Helmsley Hotels, came from a humble background. She was born Leona Mindy Rosenthal in Marbletown, just north of New York City, to Polish immigrant parents. She was brought up in Brooklyn, and although she claims to have attended college and worked as a successful model, there are no records to be found of either of these achievements. Helmsley later changed her name to Roberts and weathered two unsuccessful marriages. Two years after joining a New York real estate agency as a secretary in 1962, the tough Brooklyn broad became a broker. Within a few years she became one of New York's few self-made millionairesses by taking advantage of conversions of apartment buildings to condominiums. In 1970 the ambitious businesswoman met Harry Helmsley, a New York real estate magnate who was once one of America's richest men. The couple married two years later, after Harry left his wife Eve with a reputed $7 million settlement and Leona promised to lose 20lbs.

They quickly joined the New York social life and proceeded to buy a Manhattan penthouse as well as a twenty-eight-room Connecticut estate, a Palm Beach condominium and a private jet. But since Leona's conviction, the society friends they once catered to have deserted them.

Leona began to gain her reputation as a monster of an employer when she decided to go back to work in 1980 and became president of the Helmsley twenty-six-hotel empire. Although her advertising campaign depicting her as a meticulous boss proved effective, her employees did not appreciate her dictatorial management style. The hotel's motto was: "The only Palace in the world where the Queen stands guard." But this queen was not a kindly one. She fired one waiter for having dirty fingernails and another for having a trembling hand when he served her. When an unpaid contractor complained that he needed to feed his six children, Leona answered: "Why doesn't he keep his pants on, he wouldn't have so many problems." While giving a writer an interview, Leona came across a wrinkled bedspread and tilted lampshade and started screaming: "The maid's a slob! Get her out of here. Out! Out!" But despite this reputation as an insufferable employer, the stars booked in, including Frank Sinatra and arms dealer Adnan Kashoggi. Leona, worried about looking aged, enhanced her publicity photos with a computer to take decades off her face and inches off her figure.

She began to have delusions of grandeur – some likened Leona during this period to Marie Antoinette – and took up swimming in her penthouse pool as exercise. A liveried servant held a silver platter of cocktail shrimps at one end of

---

Pools have been running in Britain for many years, and for all who have realized their dreams and won millions, there are not many "winners" like Vivian Nicholson, who frittered the money away in record time. Nicholson's husband Keith won £152,319 in the pools in 1961 – a huge sum then. His wife went wild and blew the winnings on clothes, parties, booze and race horses. When her husband died in a car crash, what little money was left disappeared. She eventually went through three husbands, a few cruises and a pink Mercedes. Nicholson later wrote a book on her experiences titled "*Spend, Spend, Spend*", which was adapted into a television play and later into a low-budget musical. She now lives in a council flat in Leeds.

the pool and as Leona completed each lap she would clap her hands and say: "Feed the fishy." Whereby the servant would reach down and feed her a shrimp. Unfortunately for Helmsley, her new digs will not include a pool nor a servant.

Rock star Mick Fleetwood, leader of the highly successful pop group Fleetwood Mac, blew his fortune on houses, expensive toys, women and cars. He filed for bankruptcy in 1984 with debts of more than $3.7 million. Fleetwood had to give up his houses, his cars, much of his musical equipment and his huge toy collection. His lawyer told *Rolling Stone* magazine that his client was a lover of great drums, cars, beautiful women and magnificent pieces of real estate. It was his passion for buying property, however, that put Fleetwood in the red. His problems began when he purchased some real estate in Australia in 1980. But after living there for three weeks, the rock star decided that life "Down Under" was not for him, and sold the house, taking a great loss. Unfortunately he had used his house in Beverly Hills as collateral for the purchase. The next year he bought a house in Malibu he called the "Blue Whale". He took out a second mortgage on his home, but was paying $20,000 a month in payments due to soaring interest rates. Eventually his small empire started to crumble; his investments failed and his annual earnings dropped to a third of what they had been (over $1 million a year). And Fleetwood was left with almost nothing.

Scandals

William Randolph Hearst

The great newspaper magnate William Randolph Hearst was a millionaire for most of his life until, at the age of seventy-five and mired in the depression of the 1930s, he went bankrupt. But by the time World War II arrived, his fortune had been restored and when he died in 1951 at the age of eighty-eight, he left behind a legacy of tens of millions of dollars. He is remembered as one of the most influential American newspaper proprietors who helped mould the world's Press and created the phenomenon of yellow journalism.

The son of a millionaire, Hearst amassed two fortunes and at the height of his success owned forty newspapers and magazines, international news, feature and film services, and controlled several radio stations. He was born in San

---

British TV star Ted Rogers, who formerly hosted a popular game show called 3–2–1, has lost his £1 million fortune. Rogers wept with shame as he told a British tabloid how a disastrous business venture left him "stony broke". He said he also cried when his showbiz friends offered to bail him out. Since surviving his debt ordeal in 1992, Rogers has lost his house, his Mercedes, and his earning power. The comedian once regularly played polo with Prince Charles and was a friend of ex-Prime Minister Margaret Thatcher. He quit his hit show in 1988 when he decided to form his own TV production company, WRTV, with two friends. By the time the recession hit, Rogers was penniless and the business was a failure.

Francisco in 1863 to Phoebe and George Hearst, who had escaped extreme poverty to become a multi-millionaire and a US Senator for California. The couple doted on their only child. When William Randolph Hearst left Harvard University at the age of twenty-two without a degree, his father acquiesced to his request for the San Francisco Examiner, which he had been losing money on for years. To begin with, his son lost a fortune on the paper. But he managed to turn it around several years later, making it self-supporting and highly successful, when it began covering crimes and scandals and made personalities its speciality. After convincing his mother to give him a large portion of the fortune his father left her (George Hearst left nothing to his son when he died), William Randolph migrated to New York and purchased a second-rate sheet he named the *New York Journal* for £36,000. He spent a fortune luring the best known journalists away from the city's other newspapers.

The *Journal* appealed to the less literate masses and Hearst became known for championing the plight of the poor. Though hated by intellectuals, Hearst was neither stupid nor stingy, but rather a highly intelligent and energetic man who was frequently generous and a patron of public causes. He was criticized for spreading what was known as "yellow journalism" across the country. The term was coined by a cartoon strip he had purchased, and did not mean merely sensational journalism, but outright lies. His newspapers deliberately falsified the news – and some of the stories he and his journalists made up were so shocking that congressional investigations were held – and advocated the practice of public character assassination. Hearst was a tyrant as an employer whose demands were never disputed, but was considered generous in dealing with his editors and managers. He knew every aspect of the newspaper business, including the mechanical side and could master any new machinery without effort. He had a good sense of popular newspaper technique and was considered an excellent newspaper writer. Hearst also had a good publicity sense: "Putting out a newspaper without promotion is like winking at a girl in the dark — well-intentioned but ineffective," said the magnate.

Soon, Hearst spread his influence to daily papers in Boston, Chicago, Los Angeles, Pittsburgh, Detroit, Baltimore, Atlanta, Omaha, and elsewhere, eventually becoming the largest newspaper proprietor in the United States. He also published a New York daily in German and sold features to a syndicate of over 2,000 American newspapers. A powerful newspaper politician, Hearst was an ineffectual political politician who failed in his bid for Governor of New York State and never realized his dream of becoming president of the United States. After overcoming his early fear of speaking in public, he was elected as a Congressman, a job at which he proved rather incompetent. Still, his experience in politics helped him to develop a talent for blunt, fervid speeches, though he sometimes declared himself a Democrat, and other times a Republican. At the turn of the century he was considered one of America's leading liberals. He later used his considerable influence as a publisher to help bring about the Spanish-American War as a way to publicize his newspapers and himself. He sent a young correspondent, Frederick Remington, to Havana to cover "the war". Remington telegraphed to his boss: "There is no trouble here. There will be no war. I wish to return." Hearst answered: "You furnish the pictures and I'll furnish the war." He later went to Cuba to report on the war himself.

With no stock-holders or lenders to influence him, he had total power over what was written in his papers. He often used his publications to serve his beliefs and principles, and tried to stop the US from entering both World Wars. Though he was branded a traitor and unpatriotic and lost millions in revenue and thousands of readers, Hearst refused to back down. Though he gained the reputation for being a fascist when he would not support fighting in World War II, he was far from that and told Hitler during their one meeting that he was out of luck as long as he persisted in his anti-Semitism.

Hearst newspapers were highly successful until after World War I, when fierce competition from the tabloids began to eat into his circulation. In 1937 the *New York American* stopped publication after losing £200,000 the previous year. Hearst began to sell off his treasures in order to save his businesses. His holdings included an estate he built near San Francisco he named Wintoon — a Bavarian village which boasted timbered chalets where Hearst and his wife strolled in tyrolean hats. When he tired of that place, he went on to build San Simeon (Xanadu in the film *Citizen Kane*) on 200,000 acres in the Santa Lucia Mountains between San Francisco and Los Angeles. Hearst like to call it La Cuesta Encantada (The Enchanted Hill) or The Ranch. But the place was a palace, furnished with an array of treasures including Charles I's bed, statues, a Spanish monastery which he had shipped over in a crate and disassembled but never used because there was nowhere to fit it, three guest houses — one Moorish and two Spanish Renaissance, and a Swiss chalet wooden balcony which complemented a Gothic porch and several Mexican cupolas. One volume of the inventory of antiques in the house lists 6,776 items. Movies were shown in the private cinema. He had private railway trains built to carry his guests to San Luis Obispo, where one of his thirty-five cars would transport them to San Simeon on the six miles of private highway which criss-crossed his property. Hearst was an animal lover, and San Simeon featured a zoo and had wild animals freely roaming the grounds. Mouse-traps were banned from all his castles. Hearst Castle, as it is now known, is the most visited tourist destination in California. It took twenty-seven years and $8 million to build, and was designed by Julia Morgan, the first woman to graduate from the Ecole des Beaux Arts in Paris as an architect.

Briton William George Stern was a tycoon with
the dubious honour of holding a world record
for the largest bankruptcy – he lost
£104,390,248. Stern, however, was one step
ahead of his creditors and had placed his house,
his paintings and his Rolls-Royce under the
ownership of his family trust, placing them out
of their reach. The former millionaire agreed to
pay £6,000 a year to settle his debts, which
would leave some of his creditors waiting
seventeen thousand years to be paid off.

Hearst had her turn what was once a modest Spanish mission into a megalomaniac fairytale castle which they both considered a museum of architecture.

P. G. Wodehouse, who once visited Hearst at San Simeon, wrote a description of it to a friend in 1931: "The ranch – ranch, my foot; it's a castle . . . Hearst collects everything, including animals, and has a zoo on the premises, and the specimens considered reasonably harmless are allowed to roam at large. You are apt to meet a bear or two before you get to the house, or an elephant, or even Sam Goldwyn. There are always at least fifty guests staying here . . . You don't see Hearst till dinnertime . . . He's a sinister old devil, not at all the sort I'd care to meet down a lonely alley on a dark night."

Hearst had spent nearly $50 million on his collection, until he ran out of money and had to start selling pieces off. Today his treasures would be worth billions of dollars. He also sold off many of his other art treasures which were stored in five guarded warehouses in New York and used to furnish his homes there. The sale of the objects, including tapestries of four centuries, Greek sculptures, silver, furniture, armour, and paintings by Rembrandt, Hals, and Van

Dyck brought in £3 million. He also sold off property he held in Wales – St Donat's Castle, which dated back to the eleventh century and which he had purchased in 1925 despite being fervently anti-British. He had enlarged the castle – one of seven he owned – at a great expense, while ruining old buildings elsewhere in Great Britain. Hearst also owned fruit ranches, a gold mine in Idaho and two yachts, one of which he never used.

The start of World War II – wars were good for Hearst though he was an isolationist – turned his newspaper business around again after having weathered huge deficits. Soon all of the publisher's properties were bringing in profits and Hearst was able to resume his old way of life. Though his methods of journalism were rather unsavoury, he was respected for searching out iniquities of every kind, which had a deterrent effect on corporate and individual injustices, making him a public watchdog of sorts. Yet, when he set up a newspaper business in Chicago, he employed gangsters to ruin the delivery of competing newspapers and beat up their distributers. It is said that Hearst and his competitors laid the foundation for organized crime by employing these hit men. By the time the battle had ended, twenty-seven people were dead and gangsters were established. It was also widely believed that Hearst had murdered someone on his yacht, though the allegations were never proved. When the US declared they would enter World War II in July 1940, Hearst warned that the action was a "calamity" and predicted that the winner of the war would be Russia.

Hearst had become a larger-than-life character to the American people: Orson Welles based his classic film "Citizen Kane" on the life of newspaper magnate William Randolph Hearst, who tried to buy and destroy the film. When that didn't work he tried to blackmail the cinemas not to show it (though he never saw the film), a characteristic Hearst move. Though Hearst's son, William Randolph

Scandals

Hearst Junior, denies that his father tried to have the film suppressed, it is known that Louis B. Meyer tried to buy Citizen Kane and dispose of it. Orson Welles was put on Hearst's black list, which consisted of 2,000 people who were banned from his newspapers, radio stations and wire services. Citizen Kane went on to win the Oscar in 1941 for best film. Welles was not the only one to portray him in film and literature; Aldous Huxley bases his eccentric treasure collector Joseph Stoyte in "*After Many a Summer*" on Hearst.

The great publisher died in August 1951 at the age of eighty-eight. He had been nursed for several years by his long-time mistress, the actress Marion Davies, who was asleep at his bedside when he died. While she slept, two of Hearst's sons carried their father's body away and when Davies awoke he was gone. His affair with Davies, a comedy actress who had starred in silent films and was forty years his junior, was said to harm Hearst's reputation in politics for leading a "loose" private life. Davies, who was faithful to Hearst until he died, became so wealthy from all his generous gifts that she was able to lend him $1 million ($25 million today) to help him recover from the Depression when his businesses fell into a slump.

Today the remainders of the original Hearst family fortune is said to be worth between $4–$5 billion. And the film based on his life which he tried so hard to have suppressed has become even more famous than him.

Titles in the World Famous series

World Famous Cults and Fanatics

World Famous Scandals

World Famous Strange Tales and Weird Mysteries

World Famous Crimes of Passion

World Famous Unsolved Crimes

World Famous Catastrophes